Alexander Clark

**The Old Log School House**

Furnitured with incidents of school life, notes of travel, poetry, hints to teachers

and pupils, and miscellaneous sketches

Alexander Clark

**The Old Log School House**
*Furnitured with incidents of school life, notes of travel, poetry, hints to teachers and pupils, and miscellaneous sketches*

ISBN/EAN: 9783337011314

Printed in Europe, USA, Canada, Australia, Japan

Cover: Foto ©ninafisch / pixelio.de

More available books at **www.hansebooks.com**

Alexander Clark

**The Old Log School House**
Furnitured with incidents of school life, notes of travel, poetry, hints to teachers and pupils, and miscellaneous sketches

ISBN/EAN: 9783337011314

Printed in Europe, USA, Canada, Australia, Japan

Cover: Foto ©ninafisch / pixelio.de

More available books at **www.hansebooks.com**

THE

# OLD LOG SCHOOL HOUSE.

FURNISHED WITH

Incidents of School Life, Notes of Travel, Poetry, Hints to Teachers and Pupils, and Miscellaneous Sketches.

ILLUSTRATED.

"Papers—books! it makes me sick,
To think how ye are multiplied;
Like Egypt's frogs, ye poke up thick
Your ugly heads on every side."

BY
ALEXANDER CLARK,
EDITOR OF "CLARK'S SCHOOL VISITOR."

PHILADELPHIA:
J. W. DAUGHADAY, PUBLISHER,
NO. 1308 CHESTNUT STREET.
BLAND, MEYERS & WOODBURY,
INDIANAPOLIS, IND.

Entered according to Act of Congress, in the year 1864, by

## J. W. DAUGHADAY,

in the Clerk's Office of the District Court in and for the Eastern District of Pennsylvania.

TO MY FATHER,

## SAMUEL CLARK,

A HUMBLE, DEVOTED, AND FAITHFUL

## "SCHOOL-MASTER,"

THIS VOLUME IS RESPECTFULLY DEDICATED, AS A TRIBUTE OF AFFECTION AND ESTEEM,

BY THE AUTHOR.

# PREFACE.

THE story of the Old Log School House is founded on fact. The prominent characters in the narrative will be recognized by a few who may peruse these pages. Should the reader expect to find this a mere historical record of the very happenings in any particular school-house, he will be disappointed. Although we have kept in view the actual events of a special locality, yet we have designedly omitted the real names of the actors, and have not observed the exact order of their occurrence. The impartial reader will, we trust, willingly pardon these digressions.

The hopes, the fears, and the joys of a teacher's life are often strangely blended, and mark their significance upon the susceptive natures of the young by a thousand manifestations. A tender word, breathed out from a warm and loving heart, will make an impression, even upon the cheerless frost-surfaces of the great outer world; but the unspoken words of a printed page, are less sympathetic always. However, should our brother or sister teachers here discover any experiences that may revive fond memory,—or the thoughtful pupil a single sentence that may be cheering or suggestive,—we shall be satisfied. We entertain a hope, therefore, that even these unworthy pages may not have been written entirely in vain.

It may be proper to add furthermore, that the several fugitive sketches which compose the greater portion of this volume, have been collected by a personal friend, from our miscellaneous published writings, and from Manuscripts prepared at leisure hours. Hence, the variety in sentiment and style. This may serve to relieve the book from the monotony that accompanies tedious tale-telling or speculative theorizing.

To our friend and former school-mate, MR. WILLIAM H. LAWRENCE, of Hammondsville, Ohio, we are indebted for the ambrotype from which the frontispiece is engraved.

With only these words of apology and grateful acknowledgment, we respectfully submit this, our first book, to a kind and courteous public.

ALEXANDER CLARK.

# CONTENTS.

### CHAPTER I.
A Good Day's Work—The Lame School-Master—The Three R's......... 9

### CHAPTER II.
The Farmer—The Little Scholar—An unfortunate Life................... 19

### CHAPTER III.
The Distillery—Spelling-Schools—A Hard Winter........................ 26

### CHAPTER IV.
A Time of Sorrow—The Missing Scholar—Under the snow............. 35

### CHAPTER V.
The "Yallah Dog"—The Dandy Teacher—Barring Out................... 43

### CHAPTER VI.
A Sad Parting—The New Minister—The Frozen Hand.................. 53

### CHAPTER VII.
Snares and Pit-falls—Temperance Meetings—Funny Letter-Box......... 62

### CHAPTER VIII.
The New Mistress—Lame Teacher again—A Dual Death................ 71

### CHAPTER IX.
The Lazy School-Master—"Boarding Round"—Robbing a Grave...... 79

### CHAPTER X.
Suspicions and Superstitions—A Sad Farewell—New Post-Office......... 90

### CHAPTER XI.
"The Minister's Wooing"—Good News—Leather and Latin.............. 100

### CHAPTER XII.
The Inebriate—The Will—The Visit—Death of the Minister............ 108

### CHAPTER XIII.
The Quaint Letter—Riches and Honor—Conclusion...................... 120

Life Musings................................................................... 131
Summerings in Canada....................................................... 134
To a Departed Mother........................................................ 151
Visit to the Mammoth Cave.................................................. 153
My Early Home................................................................ 161
Visit to Kentucky.............................................................. 163

## CONTENTS.

| | PAGE |
|---|---|
| An Acrostic for Adela | 168 |
| A Summer Ramble | 169 |
| The May Time | 174 |
| Up the Hudson | 176 |
| Stanzas | 181 |
| On the Mountain | 183 |
| Honor thy Father and Mother | 185 |
| Laziness | 192 |
| Tobacco Teachers | 195 |
| Vicious Literature | 198 |
| June and its Teachings | 201 |
| Autumnals | 203 |
| Prize Fighting | 205 |
| Barring Out | 207 |
| An Ugly Habit | 209 |
| To the Comet | 211 |
| Teachers' Conventions | 213 |
| Fishing | 215 |
| "Away Up High" | 217 |
| Little Believers | 219 |
| My Sister's Grave | 221 |
| The Love of Christ | 223 |
| Summer | 226 |
| In Memory of Emma—A Pupil | 227 |
| Honest Willie | 230 |
| How do you Learn? | 232 |
| How do you Teach? | 234 |
| Courage, Teacher! | 236 |
| Contrasted Similes | 238 |
| 'Tis Sweet to Remember | 240 |
| Quit That | 242 |
| Christmas Time | 244 |
| Called from the Forest | 246 |
| Going Through the World | 249 |
| Contentment | 254 |
| Chirography | 255 |
| The Teacher's Position | 257 |
| A Night of Gloom | 259 |
| Winter | 269 |
| Valley Forge | 270 |
| Tippecanoe | 277 |
| Yellow Creek | 283 |

# THE OLD LOG SCHOOL HOUSE.

## CHAPTER I.

"Those years! those years! those naughty years!
　Once they were pretty things;
Their fairy footfalls caught our ears,
　Our eyes their glancing wings.
They flitted by our school-boy way;
We chased the little imps at play.

They flashed above us love's bright gem
　They showed us gleams of fame:
Stout-hearted work we learned of them,
　And honor more than name.
Well,—give the little years their way;
　Think, speak, and act the while;
Lift up the bare front to the day,
　And make their wrinkles smile;
They mould the noblest living head—
They carve the best tomb for the dead."

THERE were clamorous wants which were too beseeching,—even imperative in their utterances to be refused—wants wholly physical it is true; but nature asserts her rights, and makes her demands heard to the utter exclusion of all other cries, and so the earth was made the source of all expectation for years, and when it had in part satisfied the cravings of its dwellers, other wants found space in the realm of sound for a hearing.

Pioneers in our Western country—and they were a heroic class of men—were forced to coax and pet the earth for a subsistence even, with little opportunity for listening to the begging of the intellect for a morsel of food; but the dawning smile of plenty rested their weary hands, and thought took the throne of toil and asked for its share in life, and it came, though strangely bestowed. Knowledge was content to inhabit very singular positions, and found its way into very humble temples; but its glory was not dimmed, but rather intensified by its quaintly garnished surroundings.

The scattered families who had leveled the huge trees, drawn the immense roots, and with strong hands held the plough through the deep furrows, while mothers and daughters had woven and fashioned not ungraceful, though very coarse and strong garments, began to feel that there were other famines besides the want of bread,—other, and as insatiable longings when there was time to listen to them, as the call for food and warmth. There must be a place where the little ones could be gathered for instruction, and the older people brush the mould of forgetfulness from their earlier cultivation, and so it came to pass that with this sudden thought rushing over the community like a blaze over a prairie, they gathered for a single social day, and with quick hands reared The Old Log School House.

Just one day!

We may congratulate ourselves that the present time is speedy in the perfection of the world's work, but hardly would a hundred days serve for the erection of a school-house now. But with hands skilled by necessity, the twilight found a rude but strong temple for knowledge perched upon the corner where the roads crossed, and the fences hedged in an orchard on one side, while on the other, a forest deep, and densely covered with the green and golden mosses of centuries, grew dark in rank foliage farther away down the valley.

It had been a day of merriment, for not often did the thinly spread population assemble for any purpose, and there were interested and questioning faces to scan for answers that never shaped themselves into words. These isolated people had lost or laid aside the uses of sympathetic language; but the merry, jubilant expressions of strong natures bubbled up and ran over with laughter, and, ah! we are sorry to say it,—with the wild gaiety of the cup that leaves a bitter remembrance for the morrow!

No corner-stone was laid; no set speeches enlivened the occasion. The gallons of whisky, and the dollars in money, appropriated to the enterprise were about equal! Could the hardy settlers have looked forward with prophetic vision some fifteen years to the time when the first Temperance Meeting was held within those timber walls,—or still farther into the future, even to the present day, and viewed the changes that have been wrought in the neighborhood, how wondrous the revelation! Woody wilderness then is fruitful field to-day; drunkenness and revelry then—virtue and temperance now. Where the holy Sabbath was then profaned by hunting and fishing, the word of God is now proclaimed, and the sweet songs of Zion commingle with the melody of the groves, and are wafted, as if on angels' wings, to the peaceful mansions above.

Abel Winthrop was the leader of this army of hewers and fashioners of the new house. They did not select the site for the loveliness of prospect, though it might be called rather pleasant, but rather for the conveniences of access to the various interested parties. It was on a little rise of bare, yellow ground where nothing but an intellectual growth could be expected, Nature scorning such a spot for any of her herbaceous children. There was a little brook, spanned by a rude wooden bridge, which ran at the base of the hill of science, and sang its rhymes in summer, and roared its deep diapasons to the departing winter when its margins were bordered with vanishing crystals, and tearful, velvety snows, and it was swollen with an affluence of water.

The house was but eighteen feet square, with a low, rough ceiling, unwhitened and unadorned with the least hint at art or luxury. There were six small nine-light windows, near enough to the ground to permit the children to feast their curious eyes on the traveler who at very long interims passed that way, and it was with quite an excited throb of the young pulse, that a new face was seen, bringing fanciful pictures of the outside world, whose sounds, scarce comprehended, now and then penetrated their quiet homes.

Along two of the sides of this room, with one edge fastened to the wall, ran the writing desks, fronted by long benches of oak wood without a back for the comfort of the growing bone and sinew of the children. Then there were lower benches, graduated to the physical developement of the boys and girls. A huge chimney fronted and gaped at the master, with an iron bar for its upper lip, and fire dogs lolling their tongues of flame that lapped up Jack Frost, and swallowed him down like an anaconda, those cold winter mornings. This great gray fire-throat arched outward, with its coating of mortar and its bones of stone, and occupied a portion of the yellow barren ground, leaving the room perfectly square. Such monstrous logs as hissed, and smoked, and cracked their lives away in ruddy gleams and glorious warmth!

The external appearance of the house was not unlike that of most other buildings in the surrounding country, but it would look quaintly *zebraish* to modern architects. Byzantine, Romanesque, and Gothic styles, would here find very little upon which to lavish mediæval enthusiasm. In fact, it was essentially back-wood-ish, but the subtle influences of truth and the spirit of progression were at work, and though smouldered somewhat by the heretofore actual of their lives, yet they were destined to flame forth from this unique temple, and light many another altar of knowledge.

The door-way was small and deep of necessity, because the oaken and mortar walls were so thick, and the threshold, sloping outward as if prophetic of the many it would pour forth into the world to better its inhabitants, is now worn to thinness by the footfalls of so many pilgrims to and from its altar.

And so the second day found the creation of this striped house of rough brown bark and white plaster almost complete and ready for its uses.

It was a merry day that saw it lifted into existence, too merry, alas! with the tempting glasses of sparkling drink; and though the rearing of the Log School House was like planting abundantly for a coming harvest, yet there were tares sown that day which some time would be gathered with much weeping.

And the master!

Oh, but he was a goodly soul! One of those persons who reconcile one to the seemingly unequal bestowal of good gifts. He was an older brother of the chief of the party who, in one day, reared the house, and his name was Nelson Winthrop. In all the wide country there was no such learned man as he, though there might have been many, for he gathered to himself his great store of knowledge in the long cold evenings before the blazing pine-knot fires of his father's own hearth, while his brother, with a perfectly complete physical organization, was finding his elixir of life in a wild run of three or four miles to some *near* neighbor to pass a genial evening.

Abel was a handsome man; at least with his pleasant, animated face and fine figure, he would be called so in those days of admiration for muscle. He was warm-hearted and generous, and for the world he could not say no to the appeal of a friend. In that one tiny word *no* is rolled his destiny—is embodied his sentence for this world. He was his own only enemy, and we hope God loved him and forgave him his injuries to his own soul at last, though there was no token left that he received a Christian's inheritance.

But the master! It is pleasant to repeat his name. When he was a little lad, a great trouble came upon him and left its bitterness with him through life. He was made by an incurable disease a cripple always. Not that the affliction was unbearable, for he could walk after a time without his crutches; but there were moments when he would have envied the athletic pleasures of his brother, but for the consolation of his beloved books. His father, with a tenderness which all afflicted children inspire, would forego any happiness,—make any sacrifice to procure this exquisite enjoyment for Nelson, and so the sorrow of this one lad has made many a home and heart beautiful and happy by the mental light that came because of the physical shadow upon Nelson himself. He will see—perhaps he did and was comforted—that this was to be his burden in this life.

By the assistance of Lexicons and Grammars he mastered three languages, and with exquisite accuracy and neatness, translated portions of the New Testament into them for the use of his children. He had an unusually fine voice, and studied music, and often made the social circle glad with his own and the mingled voices of his pupils. He learned, or rather his ingenuity assisted him to make the better specimens of the household furniture of the neighborhood, beside which employment he owned a small farm that he managed, by exchanging work with his friends, to get tilled. He was one of those people on whom nature was lavishly bountiful in her gifts. If she took from him swiftness and elegance of motion, she must have given him patience and gentleness of spirit, for there were few examples of that meekness of manner for him to imitate, and which more than any other possession gives personal power.

This humble Christian gentleman dedicated to its primary uses the house, so like, and yet so unlike, Jonah's gourd. O, but it was a gala day to young hearts! A strangely fateful day to many a blossoming life! whose fruit, gathered from the Tree of Knowledge, should be good or evil to an intenser degree by this first culture. So Protean was master Winthrop's genius, that he seemed capable of comprehending the individuality of every child in his care, and of bringing to perfection the highest and best capabilities of its nature. He possessed a sort of Fata Morgana power of showing to each young life its many phases, and holy uses, and purposes.

But to the first morning!

For so its importance taught the children to call it for days afterward. It was a sparkling one in autumn, when the red and amber wine of the year was poured over the foliage by day, and the night dews glistened in silver in the morning,—when the harvest of nuts began to glint through their robings with a promise of a speedy fall,—when the brook under the bridge began to rise over the pebbles in its path with a busier and less silvery purl,—that was the one.

It was with a sort of awe that the children, tall and short, gathered in compact clusters at a respectful distance from the door, as master Winthrop came down over the hill from the southward, toward the schoolhouse, leading his little brown-eyed daughter, whose long, glossy curls and ruddy cheeks were such a promise of health, —and a son, a little shy fellow, with a prophecy of thoughtful manhood written on his still babyish face. Like a priest the master entered the house and lit the fires,—sacred those daily fires are now in many a memory,—with his two little ones standing on either side with mute wonder as to the next proceeding in the new life. After a little the fire leaped up and roared from its red lungs, and its glow crept over the wide room, giving it a touching of delicate roughness, and then the master with a wonderful self-possession, it seemed to his pupils, approached the window, and with a steady hand, rapped three distinct times upon the little nine-lighted sash, and took his seat. However common-place this event became afterward, on this morning it seemed like something wonderfully strange—indeed almost unearthly to them, and they obeyed the summons with the utmost solemnity, save here and there a nervous child who smiled with an unmeaning show of white teeth, as excitable grown people sometimes do to this day.

The boys took one side of the room, and the girls the other; the tallest at the writing-desks, and the trundle-bed sort on the benches, with their faces towards each other. Then with deep solemnity in his voice the master folded his hands and said, "Let us pray." It was not a prayer of the usual modern form, but one just suited to that still autumnal morning, and the young immortals school-housed for the first time. True it had "many an Oriental symbol and Hebrew Paraphrase;" but it was touching and subduing in its pathos and power. Those soft minor tones of its utterance touched lovingly outward to the tenderest spot in every listening heart, and upward on wings of faith to heaven's throne went the earnest beseechings of that humble teacher's soul, although the little band there assembled could not comprehend its mysterious meaning. After a slowly uttered *Amen*, the first stir was heard in the new house; and the pupils one after another came forward to exhibit their stock of school-books, which had mostly been roused from a long slumber in the bottoms of chests where precious family possessions were treasured away; and they were as divers in name as they were in number. Scarce two were alike in all the house. From the whole area of English sound and mode of speech, they seemed gathered, but it was the whole stock and must be made available. The master had never heard, happy man! of agents from Publishing Houses who bring the best text-books ever printed to be exchanged without charge for the musty, wood-covered, antiquated essence of dead brains, with only a glimmer of supernatural vitality left in them!

Each child was apportioned his lessons for the day, to be heard separately, from their precious store of books, except dear little Mary Winthrop, who held a tiny tome of manuscript, neatly bound and paged as a book, and printed with a pen by the cunning hand of her father, and which held facilities of learning years in advance of the time when he became master of the first school on the Ridge.

There were tall boys who had learned "readin', ritin', and 'rithmetic" from their mothers, and looked with not a little contempt upon the *uneducated* portion of the school.

## CHAPTER II.

"If the darkened heavens lower,
　Wrap thy cloak around thy form;
Though the tempest rise in power,
　God is mightier than the storm.
Holy strivings nerve and strengthen,
　Long endurance wins the crown;
When the evening shadows lengthen,
　Thou shalt lay the burden down."

BENNY ROLLIN was the farthest advanced in his lessons, because, perhaps, he had no father and no mother, and sorrow drives many a one to books. He was in the family with another lad of his own age—a lad whose father called more acres his own than any other man for miles around. This man, John Haxton, had taken this boy from the grave of his mother, with a little appearance of assumption, making all the sympathizing neighbors feel that by his wealth he claimed possession of the child, and intimating too, that he was the only man that could care for him properly. There was a small clearing which belonged to the lad, but it was so barren that the more he possessed the poorer he became. He had gone home with Mr. Haxton in the torpor of terrible grief, uncaring what would happen to him, and when time, that blessed healer of griefs, soothed him a little, he did not see any way of finding a pleasanter home immediately, and so there he was still.

Charlie Haxton comprehended and partook to a very disagreeable degree his father's ridiculous assumption of superiority. He was a doggëd fellow, and nothing but the marvelous self-control of Benny kept them from hostility. Benny could work faster and neater than Charlie, but the latter consoled himself with the fact that he escaped from many irksome duties by Benny's dispatch. But this morning, it was a bitter thing for the proud fellow to bear when Benny was declared to be by far the most capable scholar in the Log School House! And before pretty Mary Winthrop, too! He turned his angry face toward the little girl, and though her eyes were on the manuscript, he saw a pleasant look lighten them perceptibly, and the unconscious smile upon her young face showed subtle delight. How he wished the house had never been built!—wished his father had not been such a fool as to give the miserable yellow ground on which it stood!—wished even that Benny had been put in the grave-yard with the rest of the Rollins! He never once thought he could by any possibility attain to Benny's standing; but with the usual meanness of narrow souls, blamed some other one with his own failures.

There were the three Gordons, Annette, Lizzie, and a brother Tom, older than his sisters. They lived almost back of the forest, and two miles from the school. They were great-hearted, great-featured, coarse children, with strong, though untutored wills, endowed with marvelous fidelity to their friends, and capable of almost any amount of hatred to those they disliked. These traits were common to the three, in an apparently equal division, which fact was a marvel to master Winthrop when they first came under his supervision, but was afterward explained upon the most natural of principles. Then there was Priscilla Allen, who passed by the pet cognomen of "Silly," which name was not the least inappropriate. Her mother was of French extraction, and retained her inheritance of national love of adornment; and the limited means of its gratification, narrowed by remoteness from a town, and the scarcity of money, made its manifestations very ludicrous. She always dressed in a grotesque style, which in her own estimation, lifted her not a little in the scale of civilization and refinement, and gave her "sublime indifference" to passing criticisms. Tiny Walton was the *little* girl of the small school, and the humanizing element in the house. Not that Mary Winthrop was not as lovely, but she was not so small, and pale, and helpless; besides being the master's daughter, seemed to remove her in a measure from the common elements of school-day familiarities.

One other deserves mention. It was a half-witted child of the very poorest family of the neighborhood. He was one of those pitiable creatures but little above the animal in his intellectual development. He could articulate something which served for a name for the children whom he met. He had a spaniel-like fondness for those who were kind to him, and a bull-dog savageness toward his enemies. He desired to go to school because other children did, and because it was desolate and comfortless at home, and he was wonderfully gregarious in his tastes. If he could get near enough little

Mary Winthrop to let one of her curls slip through his long thin fingers, he seemed perfectly intoxicated with a silent sort of happiness, while she, poor girl! with the human so grandly developed in her childish soul, pitied, though she shuddered in strong antipathy when he was near, and nerved herself to give him the gratification of a touch of her waving hair. Her sweet lips would tighten over her wealth of small pearly teeth, when she saw him creeping, more like an animal than a creature with a soul, toward her, but she would not let him see her shudder. There were the four children of Abel Winthrop and several others in the school-room, who, like ciphers, may or may not be useful in their way, though their generation has little for which to thank them.

After a few days of the severest labor, physical or mental, that Nelson Winthrop had ever performed, he hit upon a plan of teaching them by topics. He would make a list of questions in Arithmetic and explain their meaning, and then let the pupils think out the reasons as he kindly answered their interrogatories by asking easy questions himself, thus leading out the mind of the child, thought by thought, until a new idea was gained by every exercise of the mind. He would arrange a series of questions in Geography which would suit any country or place and everybody's comprehension, and desired his pupils to make a common library of their text-books—for there were no printed books on this study in that school for many years—and answer the questions as they could find them best explained in all, or either of their other books, for the master asked only such questions as they had facilities for ascertaining from such helps as they could summon.

Peter Dally, the poor "half-souled" boy received his daily instruction in the Alphabet, but the same letter of one day did not seem the same the next. His feeble brain did not appear to have the faculty of retaining any thing but love and hate, and these seemed to be intensified because they were so isolated in that poor head, and had no companion faculties. A creature with prisoned soul is a solemn mystery, and it is marvelous that they inspire so little sympathy and so much abhorrence and neglect. Master Winthrop made it a matter of serious study and experiment to awaken something akin to reflection and comprehension in the child, but it was very long, and a sad miracle it was too, when it happened that the glimmer entered his shadowed soul.

The buzz of voices was a never ending source of delight to the lad, and kept him quiet all day long. Indeed, when he learned the signal of dismissal and saw it given, a distressingly dolorous expression would creep down slowly over his face, and settle into a most unmitigated melancholy. But the next morning was a renewed blessing to him, poor idiotic creature! as it ought to be to us all. Master Winthrop used to talk to him, looking steadily into his restless eyes, with that tenderly modulated voice of his, until the pupils of his strange orbs would contract, and a quiet gaze would come back to meet his own. There were glimmerings of an idea in Winthrop's head, which, if circumstance—forgive the word—if Providence had favored, would have been developed into the same grand benevolence which later days have known; but he had his hands full of noble employment, and at last it will be said of him, "He did what he could." He built the fires, kept the room and hearth in scrupulous order, and though the furniture was rough and ungainly even, he permitted no disfigurement,—no manifestations of dawning artistic genius, or enthusiasm for sculpture. He had in his keeping the elements of æsthetics, which after all the practicality of the present age, and the ascendency of utilitarianism, ought to receive half the meed of praise for civilization. With the graceful surroundings of refined life, he would have been practical enough, as his habits leaned so strongly to the *Utile Dulci*, always.

In his own house where there were only the same accessions as his neighbors possessed, there was an elegance of arrangement, an air of refinement, which was felt, but could not be imitated except as the taste was cultivated, and the eye and soul learned the difference between genuine beauty and its counterfeit. So in the Old Log School House, though the long low benches were rough and ungraceful, yet the arrangement was pleasing, and there was an almost artistic effect in the grouping of the children that made them look at times very like a tableau, or a quaint picture of puritan time. In the dark, stormy, winter days when the white earth and leaden sky gave a dull grayish tint to every face, he would build such a glowing fire as would cast coruscant gleams over every young brow, and send its warm, bright glances into the dim corners of the rooom, darting under the master's desk, and away up into the crevices of the rafters, making every thing beautiful. Master Winthrop would watch its effect with a dreamy sort of satisfaction, until some extremely sublunary remark, such as, "My pen's split too far, master," called him back to the actual of his life.

## CHAPTER III.

"Contented wi' little, and cantie wi' mair,
   Whene'er I forgather wi' sorrow and care,
I gi'e them a skelp, as they're creepin' alang,
   Wi' a cog o' guid swats, and an auld Scottish sang.
\*   \*   \*   \*   \*   \*   \*   \*   \*
Blind chance, let her snapper and stoyte on her way,
   Be't to me, be't frae me, e'en let the jade gae:
Come ease or come trouble; come pleasure or pain;
   My warst word is—'Welcome, and welcome again.'"

IT is a beautiful capability that can make common events poetical, common things artistic, common affection and its manifestations romantic, and common duties lovely and pleasant to perform. This, more than any thing else outside the bare facts he imparted, did Mr. Winthrop endeavor to teach the little children. It had made his own life welcome and happy to himself, and it was the best bestowal he could leave them.

There were habits and propensities, evil,—more than that,—extremely wicked, within the circle of the Log School House' influence, and he fought them with a persistency that was truly heroic. In those isolated settlements they almost always have an abiding place, probably because the social and intellectual facilities find little time for growth, and life becomes, from necessity, so poor in pleasures which are exalted.

There was in the vicinity an old bachelor farmer, who owned a distillery and a horse-mill, where the settlers went to grind their grain, using their own horses to turn the wheel, and, in the mean time, they found it pleasant and convenient to take a glass of stimulant, and so the strange fascination for the distiller's burning beverage grew upon them till it was past resistance. Abel Winthrop was one of his victims, and the growing sin lay like a heavy weight of sorrow upon his brother.

His eldest son, Robert, would sometimes enter the school-room with a consciousness of his father's danger written in lines of pain, and intense childish mortification at the stain upon the household. He used to get close to his uncle's chair, and lean his hot forehead upon the arm he knew was strong to do good, as if he could there get courage to meet whatever fate had in reservation for him. Then the noble boy would look toward his little sisters, and rise up feeling as if he could and would brave any thing for them. Susie and Lottie Winthrop were sweet, quiet children, and Henry was a hardy, wilful little fellow, with the noblest of impulses, but one of those peculiarly restless natures which give so much maternal solicitude, and poor Robert knew and felt all this, but he thought if his uncle Nelson would only watch him, all would go well with him.

And so with such elements the first winter wound its days into the circle of the year, and there came gatherings for older people under its roof. There were spelling schools for a mingling of merriment and culture. Bashful grown up boys and girls who had secured a little of each of the three R's before they "took up land" in the West, looked across from bench to bench at each other, by the gleam of the rousing firelight, and the two weakly tallow candles which were supported in little blocks by inch auger- holes in the centre, and kept weeping oily tears until the last best speller was obliged by failure to sit down vanquished.

There were two young men, generally solicited by the master, to choose sides, and the two so honored took each a seat on either side of the mammoth fire-place, by the long writing desks, facing each other, with the power of calling to their side of the room, alternately, the one they pleased of the unappropriated and eager youngsters. The master's rod, like Aaron's, had a power in turning wondrous events in favor of or against the "captains" who appealed to it in times of verbal war. The "first choice" was awarded to the one who would be so fortunate as to get the upper hand twice out of three times in tossing up and measuring the rod, hand over hand, to the switch end. Now it so happened that these favored young gents invariably invited the girl they liked best, without any regard to the success of their party, to sit beside them; and after this was accomplished, scholarship was honored most. If the two leaders happened to be rivals, as was sometimes the case, there was a sad reluctance manifest in tossing the rod, and the discomfited bore with but little equanimity his defeat; and pretty nearly always there was a trial of strength, and courage, and muscle, at the first opportunity. If the young lady whose name was uttered did not choose to sit beside the young man, etiquette had established a law that she should not spell a word that night, and but few had the courage to manifest so palpable a regard for the young man disappointed in the first choice.

After the occupants of the house were divided, one against the other, the master gave out the hardest words he could find, first to one side and then to the other, and the party who missed lost the best scholar, and so on, until the one side gained the whole, and then there was a general shout for the victor. Sometimes the entire school rose up in their seats, and words were given them, which, if missed, the spellers were requested to seat themselves, as a signal of defeat, until there were none left standing, the last up being the champion of the district.

About mid-winter, a Scotchman came among them and bought a few acres of land adjoining the homestead of Nelson Winthrop; and as was usual, the whole community came forward to assist in the erection of a dwelling. Presently the family came, and a host of young Scots there were, too. It was astonishing to contemplate their sleeping chances in that small log cabin; and as to eating, it filled a humane mind with the most uncomfortable apprehensions. But they were stout, happy looking little Highlanders, and their broad brogue was a never ending source of amusement to the older settlers, as were the feline sounds of the *ow's* and *an's* to the emigrants. The hope of the new house, Sandy McLain, was a sturdy little fellow, with a large brain whose machinery would take an immense amount of propelling power to start into working order, but it would be marvelous in its capabilities and endurance when once moving. Often, and often, the assembled school would be convulsed by his curious eyes becoming walled with endeavoring to comprehend his teacher's explanations, and then exclaiming in an intensely pitiful tone:—

"Aweel, aweel! I'm daft an' dinna ken!"

Mr. Winthrop saw that he would "ken" by and by, and felt a prophetic stimulant in his own soul, which kept him to his task of *starting*. It is wonderful that we all feel so little awe for a child! We can not see beyond its present, nor imagine what it may be to us, and to the world hereafter. The strings upon which a teacher plays, will vibrate for ever, and throw out discord or harmony, according to the tone given to them, to bless or torment our souls here, and also in the vailed beyond.

Sandy began at the rudiments.

Indeed, he started with Peter Dally, but he ranged greatly above his companion in the estimation of his school-fellows. True, he was not repulsive in his looks, but he was droll, and had a broad, corrugated forehead, and eyes shadowed by unusual perceptive faculties, which were in a torpid state awaiting the touch of master Winthrop. So at last the winter wore away, and the school was scattered among the rural homes for a couple of months; and though the separation was with many tears on the part of some, and howlings, which were almost absurd in their intensity, from poor Peter, yet the spring sunshine brought a balm for all,—a promise of something sweet to each young soul,—though they could not have found words to tell what it might be, or what they would have if they could choose.

Benny Rollin felt keener than any the sorrow of parting, for it had been the one fond pleasure of a life-time, after all the sorrows he had borne. Now for toil and constant association with his detestable companion, Charlie Haxton! But he nerved himself to bear cheerfully, even as Nelson Winthrop did, his troubles. Mary Winthrop changed slates with him on the last day, and that, though he could not tell her how, elevated his spirits wonderfully, and notwithstanding he found it shivered to fragments in his room the next day, yet the remembrance that she *offered* to give it, comforted him not a little. He knew how and why it was done, but he would not acknowledge that he noticed it, even to Charlie. Mr. Haxton was—and not in a small degree, either—vexed that his son was so much inferior to this dependent in his household, but tried to think it was just as well, for the one *needed* brains, as he had a fortune to accumulate, and the other required nothing. To Charlie Haxton, the winter had been a miserable waste of days, but to Benny Rollin it lay in memory like an Epic poem, with little idyllic bits of beauty whose rhythm and melody were the voices of Mary Winthrop and Tiny Walton. The latter was the little muffled maiden he had drawn to and from school all winter with the tenderness and consideration of a great-hearted man. He loved the child well, and she was the only creature upon earth that he dared to ask love from, and he had it—unmeasured always. Tiny was the only daughter, and there were but two sons, mere babies, and a half-invalid father, and as meek, gentle, and loving a mother as ever blessed a child's lip with tender kisses, or followed it with prayers. Mrs. Walton often wished she might ask Benny to come to their house for a home, poor as it was in comparison to the one he had, and she knew he would gladly exchange, but it would offend

Mr. Haxton, and he held a mortgage upon their homestead.

She dared not do it.

Benny spent many evenings in the family, and Mrs. Walton possessed a few old choice books which she spared to Benny, though there was not another one in the settlement, except Mr. Nelson Winthrop, who would have been permitted to fondle them even. Kind, good, and generous as she was, these were her only intimate friends, and they were human to her, both for the instruction they gave and the consolation they afforded; and she could not risk them.

The Log School House was occupied that summer by a girl from the village sixteen miles distant, who brought very little new or good into the hearts of the children; but she initiated some of them into the mysteries of little feminine accomplishments, taught them prettier ways of arranging their sunburned hair, let the boys make saw-teeth of the edges of the benches, and write hieroglyphics upon the smooth spots of plaster and the unpainted walls and window-casings. She taught them of the violets, daisies, and sweet-williams in the woods, and awakened a love for the pretty wild children blossoming under the hedges and by the brook; and, in her ladylike way, performed her mission. Perhaps it was well for them as it was, for they had dealt too long and intimately with the actual of their lives. But when the crisp-brown leaves began to whirl in the dreary autumn winds, it made a deeper inspiration come to the breaths and a stronger bound to the pulse of the little people, to see Nelson Winthrop with his two children approach the school-house once more. It was with a curl of disgust about his lip that he surveyed his once orderly room, but he was one to bear with apparent equanimity what he could not help, after the first twinge of pain was over, and its silent expressions passed from his face.

It was a cold winter, after a summer of great heat, and drouth, and discouragement, with but a partial fulfillment of the promise of the spring, when depression seemed to be imparted even to the children, and though Mr. Winthrop with his exquisitely organized nature, and intensely sympathetic heart, felt more than any its enervating influences, yet he strove to throw off the lethargy and enter again upon his labors with renewed zeal. The winter was to have its trials. The smaller pupils had learned disorderly habits, and the awe of the school-room had partially worn off. The older boys had, some of them, been deputied to grind corn at the distiller's mill, and felt as if they were men, because the rich man had drank with them. They felt the restraint to be irksome, particularly Charlie Haxton. He had too often felt his inferiority in the presence of Benny Rollin, and even his father in his impatient moments had contrasted them in the presence of both, and his son thought he had the power of assuming the privilege of manhood first in the way of treating his friends to tobacco and whisky, and fancied the penniless orphan boy would envy him, but even in this expected pleasure he failed to find satisfaction, and he was very morose and idle. But still Mr. Winthrop had his compensating pupils—what teacher has not?—and he comforted himself with them. The sparkle of gladness which bubbled up during his first winter had died down to the clear, cold, but pure cup of his existence.

Peter Dally did not find all the attention of the previous winter, but he did not—poor boy!—seem to notice it. The Gordons were perverse, sometimes, and talked of going away to school if the crops were better next year. . However little sorrow there would be for this, on the teacher's part, every one who has been a master of a score of children, knows there is a sting in such a remark which leaves a significant pain for hours or days. But Mr. Winthrop failed not to sow the same good seed, even if the prospect of a bountiful harvest was not so brilliant.

The evening schools at which the faithful teacher labored to interest the youths in music, and with much success, to a half invalid, though willing man, proved a severe duty. His decided and oft-expressed hostility to dram-drinking and inebriation, in every form, met the opposition of some who should have hearkened to his warning, and these influences served to trouble his thoughts, when outside the dedicated six hours; but when the unusually inviting chances for frolic on the hill-slides and coasting places of gleaming ice, took the edge of discontent from his pupils, he got on better.

## CHAPTER IV.

"' My Lord hath need of these flow'rets gay,'
  The Reaper said, and smiled,
' Dear tokens of the earth are they,
  Where He was once a child.
They shall all bloom in fields of light,
  Transplanted by my care,
And saints, upon their garments white,
  These sacred blossoms wear.'"

But soon after the ushering of the New Year, fearful lung fevers ravaged the neighborhood, and left their livid touches upon at least the cheeks of one in almost every home in the district.

The hardiest seemed first stricken.

Poor Sandy McLain's brothers and sisters—seven children in all there were of them—were smitten, and three lay under the snows of midwinter in the still forest burial-place, the first garden of graves planted in that new country. Oh, but it was a sad, sad winter! Tiny Walton had been seized, but the fever had left her, and she lay like a broken lily of the valley, still and white, in the one room of her father's house, with Benny Rollin for a constant watcher. Mary Winthrop's was one of the worst cases known to the unskilled doctor, who, half-farmer, half-physician, and a great deal fool, pretended to be learned in the ways of life and death. Benny wept beside Tiny, but his face whitened and grew rigid when he was permitted to look at those long curls shorn away in a rippling heap of dusky gold on a white napkin by the bedside of Mary Winthrop, and upon those restless bright eyes which had been his courage and inspiration in the school-room—everywhere!

Peter Dally lay crouched upon the hearth in the anteroom, moaning softly, and with a deal more intelligence in his eyes than was ever there before, watching the door that led to Mary's room, to get, if possible, one glimpse at the sweet suffering face. Death seemed persistent in his attempts to bear away this child, and held his dark wings above her for days and days, and at last left her to her friends and the world, but more than all, to the miserable boy, who day after day waited and watched with the closed portals of his soul widening slowly but surely by his agonized suspense, until the human shone perceptibly out of his strange eyes. He had only now learned what death was, looking at it in the faces of Sandy McLain's brother and sisters, and watching the solemn interment under the snow, and the tears of the bereaved—perhaps the first tears, too, that he had ever seen drop from the eyes of strong men—all affected him, touched him with a softening spell that would never be cast off. He had cried, but never wept, tears seeming to belong only to a higher order of beings; but when he was made to comprehend that Mary Winthrop would not die, the tears fell from his face heavy and fast, and the stone was rolled away from the wordless, sepulchred world of his spirit, and he said, "Me be buried now—me so glad," and fainted.

Had the dumb dog on the mat spoken thus, Nelson Winthrop could not have been more startled; but he only bowed his head with this new glimmer of hope for the idiotic boy, and wept for very gladness. Two blessings like his, a spared idol and a new hope, were almost too much joy, and his spirit reveled in its affluence of happiness, and he fervently thanked the All-Father for his loving kindness and great mercy. When a few convalescing days had passed, the good man planned a visit for Peter to the sick room of his child. She had been apprized of the wonderful change in his mental nature, and seconded her father's wishes with the usual enthusiasm of tender nature. It was an amazing change that had crept over the child! He was tidier in his costume and hair; his hands were fairer for cleanliness; his figure was a tithe more erect, and his face wore a strangely expectant expression, unlike any thing seen upon it before. His poor mother, not many degrees above her boy in intellectual culture, whatever Nature had bestowed, was filled with wonder, and followed the lad on his errand to see Mary Winthrop. He had been promised a look sometime that day, and the impatience which in him had always found utterance in a howl, was only now an earnest, questioning look, with once in a while a quick gesture, indicative of mental agony.

The door was opened at last, and in imitation—he never imitated any thing before—he walked lightly and noiselessly in, and with tearful utterance said, "Mary, Mary," with perfect distinctness. She held out her hand to him, and smiled with not a shudder or quiver of a muscle. It seemed as if she had stood in the vestibule of the other world, and had learned to see as God sees, and pity such stricken souls. It was a beautiful and touching sight, and Mrs. Winthrop turned away with her full heart to be glad alone with the Bestower of all good. Poor Mrs. Dally was wordless, but she wiped her brimming eyes with Mr. Winthrop's hand, comprehending dimly that her "half-souled" child might grow to be something to her lonely life, at last, through the faithfulness of the teacher in the Log School House.

The fever abated at length, and the school was gathered in part with a subdued spirit manifest in every face. Some were not yet well, and never would be, though life might or might not linger with them for many months, perhaps years. Tiny Walton's little sled stood no more in the embrasure of the school-room door, and though no one spoke the words, all felt that when the spring beauties bloomed they would be gathered to lie by her little dead face. Benny Rollin could not study. He laid his handsome head upon his desk, and under his neatly written copy he had penned, "Dust to dust." "I am the Resurrection and the Life." "Suffer little children to come unto me, for of such is the kingdom of Heaven," and other indicative sentences, and though such a digression from duty would, at other times, be considered worthy of reprimand, yet it was passed with only a silent prayer that the lonely boy might be comforted.

It was the last week of school. There had been much accomplished in the brief time since the days during which the epidemic had closed the doors of the Log House, and Mr. Winthrop felt, on the whole, satisfied. Sandy McLain had fairly stridden into geography and arithmetic from the spelling-book, and his brogue was softening into a more delicate style of conversation. Peter Dally had actually conquered the alphabet, and was ready for the a-b-ab's. He spoke more plainly, and something unasked brushed up the great stone hearth when the brands had fallen. It was the afternoon of Wednesday when a messenger came for Benny Rollin. The poor lad's lips whitened, for he knew too well what the message meant. Even Charlie Haxton pitied him when he saw the agony creep down over brow, eyelid, and to his very chin, and his hands close convulsively, as if he would clutch at something escaping him for ever—something his dearest, best, all!

Presently he sat by the child's bed, and her thin, pretty fingers lay still and cold in his own; and her soft voice, softer than ever, as if she were so near heaven she could hear the angels talk, and keyed her tones from theirs, was speaking her last words to him, "Benny, I'm very sorry to leave you, but you know I must go; I've made you all so much trouble, and I can't ever be well any more if I stay. Shall I tell your mother when we meet how good you have always been to me? I am a little girl, only nine years old, but I have thought sometimes, when I was a big woman, and you a tall man, how glad it would make me to be good to you as mother is to father always. But somebody will love you. I think Mary Winthrop would, if you were as kind to her as you have been to me. Kiss me, Benny, I am very tired—" and she went to sleep, that sweet, lasting, dreamless sleep which comes to all sometime.

"It is good when it happens, that we die before our time," wrote the poet who had suffered, and little Tiny Walton might have learned had she lived, what too many women have before, and wakened to sorrow, even that kindness from man is not always born of that love he bestows upon his wife. It was well that she died, believing that she was all the world to her friends, as he was to her. He did not know how it was then, and sorrowed bitterly over her death, but he comprehended it all years afterward, and thanked God that she was with the angels.

It happened the last afternoon of the term—Tiny's burial, and all the pupils were there. The spring sunshine lay soft and warm over every thing, and the crimson tassels of the maple hung like ruby jewels from the trees, and the blue and white violets, and pale anemones were looking timidly up into the sky, and each child's hand plucked its sweet blossom for the delicate coffin Nelson Winthrop had made for the dead girl.* And the little waxen creature was hidden away under the springing blooms of the young year, to burst at last into the perfection of those of whom the Father makes up his jewels. Benny only, lingered by the small mound, and afterward was found at its head, a neatly carved wooden cross, marked,

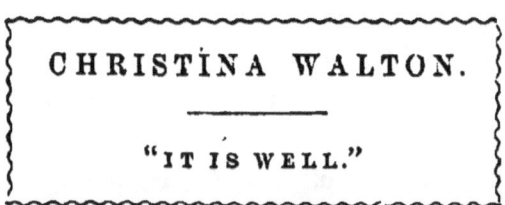

Benny Rollin was seventeen now; and this last drop in his cup of sorrow, made a man of the boy. Dear Benny Rollin! He had learned by his grief, how needful was a properly educated physician, and resolved, if

by any possibility he could, he would study medicine, and live among those who were familiar to him, and bound to him by a common suffering. Of course his companions laughed and flouted at the idea, but he was too conscious of its importance, to be sneered from his purpose, and he began a private course of classical study, under the tuition of his old and early teacher. He knew it would be very long before he completed any thing like a passable education, because of poverty and his lateness in beginning; but all these obstacles only stimulated him.

You should have seen the look on Mr. Haxton's face when the resolution was announced to him! It was a mixture of surprise and mirth, so equally divided, that it was no safe thing to hazard a guess, as to which would preponderate at last. But the idea grew upon him.

"Dr. Rollin, adopted son of J. Haxton, Esquire. It sounds well, and he is so handy—he'll get a big name. I'll get the lad all his books, and help him on, and may be it will come back in some shape. We've had enough dying here this winter, by tom-foolery. Yes, I'll help the boy. Here Benny, begin your doctor stuff to-morrow. I'll back you! May be you'll keep me out of my coffin the longer, won't you, boy?" and he gave the youth a facetious poke with his hard, stout fingers, which was any thing but funny, but had to be received as a wonderful joke. Surely Benny was grateful, but somehow his sensitive nature revolted from accepting so much from John Haxton. He knew that he had thus far more than paid his way in the strange home, and did not feel disturbed at the past—but the future! However, the boy reasoned well, though not in accordance with modern poetic independence, and consequent struggling and suffering. He said to himself:—

"John Haxton, Esquire, is not *given to giving*. He doesn't know the pleasure of such a thing. If he finds it out through me, he may do his share of good after his only fashion in the world. If I refuse to accept it, he may never try the experiment again, and of course never know how good it is. If there is a little spring of kindness pent up in his soul, it may find a larger opening with use. Yes, I'll let him be good to me."

## CHAPTER V.

> " In the silent midnight watches,
>   List—thy bosom door!
> How it knocketh, knocketh, knocketh,
>   Knocketh ever more!
> Say not 'tis thy pulse's beating;
>   'Tis thy heart of sin:
> 'Tis thy Saviour knocks, and crieth,
>   'Rise, and let me in.' "

THAT evening found him at Nelson Winthrop's house consulting about his new life, and watching the sparkle of Mary's sweet, winning eyes, whose velvety look was changed by the excitement of the great good coming to her friend. Rollin found a proper and judicious counselor now, as he had always done in Mr. Winthrop. He was, according to advice, to push on as rapidly as possible in all the sciences and the dead languages, and wait for future indications to decide for him, as to medical instruction. Mr. Haxton had no idea there was so much to be known, before he could meddle with ipecacuanha, bones, and lancets, and felt a little impatient, and perhaps frightened, that he had become responsible for so much expense; but he was not one to turn back in any thing, good or bad, that he attempted.

We must not judge the man too harshly, for we do

not know all the scars and hardened spots in his heart, caused by early pressure of want, lack of love and kindness.

Hearts, and their ways of expression and modes of doing good or ill, are like the changes of the *Ranz des Vaches* on Alpine hills, gay or sad, minor or major, according to the mood of the singer. They are always thrilling to the listener, and benevolence is always effective in some way, either to the giver or receiver, or oftener to both, and makes melody and happiness somewhere.

Benny began his Latin with Mary for a companion, and it added not a little to the pleasure of study. Young Sandy McLain used to come in softly, and finger the big books, whose words and uses he could not comprehend, but there was a hope, an expectancy even, written all over his face, that the mystery was to be solved for him.

That summer the school had a genial character for its master. A strange, elderly man he was, once a hard drinker, but now reformed, a temperance lecturer, indeed, and earnest in his influence to oppose what he knew too well was ruining the bodies and souls of many around him. He was honest, humble, and social, not so scrupulously particular in his toilet as in his love of truth. He kept a "yallah dog," a sneak of a canine, that made a daily living by stealing the children's lunch from the baskets under the benches and behind the door, which bit of irresponsible pilfering the master seemed to overlook, and the children hesitated to report to the owner of the thief, lest a worse thing might befall them.

This teacher was a good singer, and taught singing-school summer afternoons and winter nights, boarded round, and from the closest scrutiny into Scripture teach-

"He wore blue linsey-wolsey, very wide, a great brown coat, a yellow tunic of wool, and a Highland cap with an oily blue tassel." Page 45.

ings and Biblical History, came to the conclusion that Judas Iscariot was, after all the prejudices of modern men, a righteous and honest man! After such a conglomerate of nature, and acquired characteristic concomitants, no one will be surprised to know that he wore blue linsey-woolsey trowsers, very wide, a great brown coat, a yellow tunic of wool, and a Highland cap, with an oily blue tassel.

With all his quaintness of dress, and eccentricity of mind, with the remembrance of what he had been, and the constant presence of the gaunt "yallah dog," whose name was "Crusty," because he coveted crusts, he was a fair English scholar, and *everybody loved him!* He had a heart of tenderness, and was often seen to shed tears over the griefs of his friends. It was a strange school, but served to make the little people happier, if not wiser or better, after the usual mode of counting goodness or wisdom. However, it is the firm belief of the writer of this scrap of veritable history, that happiness is a civilizer, a humanizer, and a promoter of heart education, which important branch is sadly neglected now-a-days. This venerable teacher of the olden time has gone to his upper home, and has left three sons, all of whom have become teachers. Two of them have been called "master" within the walls of the Old Log School House in recent years.

For the next session another was hired, not for his fitness for the position, but because the district had grown "wise in its own conceit," and gave the school to the lowest bidder, and this was the man. As such a thing as a newspaper was scarcely an established fact, in the minds of most people thereabout, at least, by the witness of the eye, there were no "sealed proposals" advertised for through such a medium, but the Log School House door was the public vehicle of news, and announcements of all sorts, political, religious, and monetary.

Mr. Gordon was the prime mover in this advanced step in civilization, and congratulated himself not a little on this money saving arrangement. Such a gentlemanly, good-looking young man as he secured for the position, by his active exertions and financial diplomacy!

He was too fastidious to board round, and as Mr. Gordon had as ample room as any one in the district, Phelim Andrews concluded a bargain with his patron, and took lodgings immediately. How the Misses Gordon grew in importance and tawdry finery after this family acquisition! How novel and taking were the innovations in the school-room! Everybody was distracted with delight at the charming young stranger and his elegant manners! Besides, he knew *so much!* It was whispered about that he could, if he chose, speak at least a dozen different languages; but he wasn't "stuck up," and did not care to make a show of himself. Swimmingly the school went on for a while; but time and temper helped to disenchant a portion of the population, and the intense admiration he received, waned with the sympathy involuntarily bestowed upon the flogged portion of the pupils, and especially upon poor Peter, who had always been treated kindly by the masters heretofore, and had so grown in spirit that he could read tolerably, and perform many little labors for his mother, much to her delight and comfort. The house was untidy, the books no longer an object of economical care and almost reverence. A book had been hitherto a precious possession, but from this time distrustfulness crept into the progressive developments of the growing generation. Benny Rollin studied at home; so did Mary Winthrop; and Charlie Haxton's education was already finished; that is, his book culture was over, but there were fearful lessons before him, which he would get too fully by heart. Poor Charlie!

Abel Winthrop was slowly sinking, and no love, no expostulation or warning availed to stir him now. His son, his noble boy, had learned a man's grief, without its wisdom, and through it he was prudent and thoughtful to a painful degree. He was the recipient of his mother's fears and suffering, without the strength to help her, though his affectionate sympathy was the one sweet drop in the cup of her sorrow. Sometimes when he and his companions were wild with merriment, skimming over the ice, or flying down the hill from the house to the smooth, snowy surface of the brook, he would turn away from this sport in sudden remembrance. Here Phelim Andrews, Esquire, made a horizontal descent, when in the effort of seizing Peter, who was discovered in the act of wearing the master's hat, in an imitative way, upon the corner of his head, without in the least regarding Newtonian discoveries in the laws of gravitation, to the irreparable injury of the aforesaid glossy beaver. Peter never ventured to approach the school-room door again, and Mary Winthrop found a little leisure, each day, to give him a lesson. He liked that.

In those days "barring out" was a common practice among the schools of that country, and when the Christmas-day was nearing, the larger boys of the school requested the gift of a few bushels of apples from Phelim, in behalf of the school, expecting and almost wishing that he would refuse, that there might be some plausible excuse for carrying him out in derision on Christmas morning. Phelim Andrews indignantly declined acceding to the popular custom, and threatened the most summary vengeance upon any who would dare to interfere with his decision or his dignity. But the young braves were not to be frightened so easily from their cherished purpose to give Mr. Andrews a "lift," in case of mulishness; and sure enough, on Christmas-day, he was seized by a band of boys "in time of books," and triumphantly carried out-of-doors, amid the cheers of a score or two of exulting younglings, who delighted to see the master so overwhelmed with defeat and disgrace! In spite of his threats and terrible efforts to dispel the young insurrectionists, he was completely vanquished, and regained possession of the house, only when he had signed a treaty of peace, in which was granted the quantity of apples solicited, and also five gallons of sweet cider as a premium! The urchins were a little less orderly during the remainder of the session, feeling that there was a power not far off sufficient even to strike terror to the heart of the tyrant master!

When the term closed, the young man suddenly disappeared, with a promise of marriage unfulfilled with Miss Gordon, senior, and his board bill unpaid. If you think, dear reader, that Mr. Winthrop was good enough to sympathize with the sufferings of Mr. Gordon's pocket, and the family disappointment in not making a permanent relationship with the elegant teacher, you are mistaken. He could not be grieved, though he knew it was his Christian duty to be so, and endeavored to look very

"He was seized by a band of boys, and triumphantly carried out of doors, amid the cheers of a score or two of exulting younglings." Page 48.

solemn and sorry, but the corners of his finely cut mouth would curl into a smile at the thought, and Benny Rollin and Mary Winthrop made merry over the matter, and cracked many jokes about Mr. Gordon's "pheelings for Phelim."

Still Mr. Gordon persisted in his plan of bidding for a master, with that stubbornness and persistence which accompanies disappointment in very narrow minds.

Another summer and another winter wasted in this way; and then Nelson Winthrop entered the Log School House once more, with a wild welcome from the boys, and as hearty a one, though less demonstrative, from the girls. Rollin was now prepared to take a course of Medical Lectures, and he had so grown into favor with John Haxton, that the man seemed to grudge very little the seemingly large amount required for the trip, matriculation fee, and living expenses. The truth of it was, Benny always knew when there was hurry on the farm; when there was a delicate bit of work to do; or when Mr. Haxton needed the recreation of an hour's reading from some book he had never seen or heard of, and the man appreciated it. Besides, his son was getting unruly, dissipated, and idle. In truth, he was bitterly disappointed in his boy.

John Haxton's pride of possession, was somewhat abated in the humiliation of his eldest hope. His daughter was like her mother, good, orderly soul—who considered cleanliness next to godliness, and cultivated her tidy virtues to a very extreme and uncomfortable degree. Poor creature! It had no growth except that which was induced by the scrubbing brush and duster!

John Haxton was the opposite of his wife in his

habits. His theory of neatness was all right, but like a popular modern clergyman, a theory was enough to expect of one man. As might be expected, the domestic friction was constant and irritating, and the poor man found the oil of consolation alone in Benny Rollin. He had grown to be a handsome, gentlemanly fellow, and in his presence, the unbrushed boots of the head of the house were spared ungrammatical anathemas from Miss Araminta Haxton.

Perhaps this reticence on the part of the young lady may be accounted for, by a very trifling occurrence. Benny found a scrawled scrap of paper in the great, gaping fire-place, one day, on which was written and rewritten in extremely inelegant chirography, "*Mrs. Dr. Araminta Haxton,*" as if somebody was anxious to see how it would look spelled out. He did not laugh, he did not smile even, but carefully thrust it farther into the blaze, that it might be fully consumed. He was very coolly respectful to the young lady afterward, indeed extremely dignified, which led the young queen of tidiness to all sorts of explanations in regard to her opinions about love and money. Indeed, she went so far as to say, that it was her private and settled opinion, that a profession was equal to a big farm, particularly, that of a doctor. Benny said he thought so, too, and always had, which remark left her in the dark in regard to the young man's bashfulness and failure to propose.

The time came for Benny to go to Philadelphia for the winter, and the house was in a stir of preparation. He would have to wear collars every day there, and carry white pocket handkerchiefs all the time, so they had been informed, and it was with a sullen look that

Charlie watched all this preparation and extravagance, as he called it.

"Father makes a mighty fuss if I spend a little money for fun, and this pauper can have all the finery and gimcracks he wants. He can be a gentleman and I must work on the farm. We'll see how it will end—we'll see;"—and with a wicked purpose in his eyes, he started for the horse-mill, to spend the day and night.

Benny was really grateful, and expressed so much satisfaction to Mrs. Haxton, that she said one day:—

"Ben Rollin, if you don't stop your talk, I shan't be able to work your name in red cross-stitch in the corner of this 'ere pocket handkercher. You ought to have learned the preachin' business, you have got such a parsuadin' talk. I aint a mite sorry we've done such a sight for you, neither is my old man. We know it's just the same as doin' it to the family."

This winding up of her remark, was rather an ambiguous conclusion, and troubled the student not a little.

Did they think he would marry "Minta," and were they, after all, investing for their own family? Why, he would rather take "Silly" Allen, with her ridiculous taste for display, and good-natured liking for everybody who did not laugh at her style. Yet he could not speak of the questionings which so troubled him. He knew who was all the world to him, and the little, goldenly fair curl he had kept in his possession since the fever winter, would have enlightened Miss Haxton as to her prospects, if it had happened to be exposed by any mishap. But she was not so positive of her future name, as to have refused a proper offer of a house to scrub, and a husband to scold. This Benny knew, and in the possibility of an offer of marriage, from some one to her, lay all his hope of future friendship with the feminine portion of the family. He and they understood that he would not marry for several years, and perhaps the young lady would think the prefix of Dr. to her name would not pay for the procrastination of wedding cake and a house warming. At any rate Benny grew sanguine, and his spirits bubbled up and overflowed in contagious merriment. Somehow he seemed to feel certain of Mary Winthrop's regard for him, and never doubted that her future was pictured to her delicate fancies beside him. That they were to be together always, to his unquestioning heart, seemed inevitable, and very pleasant altogether. There were no words spoken, nor were there any needed, for she trusted him wholly and entirely always.

## CHAPTER VI.

*" Build to-day, then, strong and sure,*
 *With a firm and ample base;*
*And ascending and secure*
 *Shall to-morrow find its place.*
*Thus alone can we attain*
 *To those turrets, where the eye*
*Sees the world as one vast plain,*
 *And one boundless reach of sky."*

FEW women could have been thus satisfied, words are so precious to them. They hoard them and repeat them with their prayers—make their solitude musical—their monotonous lives changeable and beautiful with the remembrance of their utterance. A wife who had been loved for years with the tenderest and most unchangeable devotion said:—

"My heart craves audible expressions of affection. I could forget little irritations and small faults in my husband, with a setting of tender and affectionate words. My heart and ears crave the sound as they do sweet music, and their echoes make glad the most wearisome or painful hours."

Others crave nothing. They are consciqus of their position, and feel with an unwavering conviction that they are enthroned, and require no earthly homage.

Such was Mary Winthrop. Happy, unquestioning heart!

She did not grow tearful at the parting, nor did her smile dim, though there was a pallor, slight, but still real to the eye of Benny Rollin, over her sweet face. She kept a Roman spirit hidden under a soft exterior, and felt courage to endure any thing for her beloved, with a woman's heroism and a Christian's resignation. She was a genuine Optimist. Thank God, all ye who are, for there be few who can in truth comfort themselves with the sweet balm, so faithless are too many natures.

"I watch her as she steals in some dull room
   That brightens at her entrance—slow lets fall
A word or two of wise simplicity,
Then goes, and at her going, all seems dark.
Little she knows this; little thinks each brow
Lightens, each heart grows purer with her eyes;
Good, honest eyes—clear, upward, righteous eyes,
That look as if they saw the dim unseen,
And learned from thence their deep compassionate calm!"

"I shall miss you, Mary," said Benjamin Rollin, which sententious sentence was intended for a question, more than an assertion.

"I am sorry," she said with truthful and charming *naiveté*, "for it may retard your progress; you are so accustomed to mingle me with your books. There will be not a little strangeness for me in the new way, but my loss will be compensated to myself, by knowing how much you are learning to tell me on your return. I hope the world will look as beautiful to you as I fancy it to be, and that you will find many friends to love and care for you. Not that they will care for you as we do who know you best, but for what you seem to every one—good, honest, and *ambitious.*" That last word was emphasized slightly, and the listener felt it, and though he needed no especial stimulant, yet it was a tonic, whenever he felt weary, or loathed the details of his chosen profession.

And so they parted.

She with her reticent notion continued to live the past and future in the utter silence of her quiet life, doing the petty and wearisome duties of her isolated home, with ambition firing her veins and thoughts with a strange and quenchless flame, yet never letting an expression fall, of the fancies and purposes that glowed and vivified her whole being, except at long interims, when a partially confidential talk with her father would reveal the inner life of the half child, half woman.

With the people about her, mental torpor was a virtue. Physical torpor was the one unpardonable sin. A man's character was estimated and set down in the unwritten, though perpetually legendary, annals of his time, by the amount of work he could do. A woman who could keep house on the smallest means, and look tidy and happy under the burdens of her life, ask nothing and expect nothing of the pleasurable portion of existence, was a Christian of the highest feminine order. In fact, work and contentment were the cardinal virtues of the inhabitants of the Ridge.

Mary Winthrop understood this to be their peculiar fault, and endeavored to overcome the infatuation, though with but little success. The people were disposed to be shy of the Winthrops now, and not a little envious, as they knew that they saw in their intelligent faces at least their equals.

"When a man is contented," says a modern preacher and reformer, "thoroughly contented, in the common acceptance of that questionable virtue, he is fit to be buried." No one should ever be content when there is a point still higher that he can reach—a point where any soul can look upward unabashed. Content is the bane of progress, the clog upon the feet of improvement. Never stop in attempting to gain any probable or possible good until the voice of the Inevitable says, "Hitherto, and no further."

Benjamin Rollin went to his labor that autumn, in the great city of Philadelphia, Mary Winthrop to her own home, with Sandy McLain and Peter Dally for evening pupils, while each had his duties, one in the household, one in the threshing barn, and poor Peter in the husking stack of Nelson Winthrop. The last had become quite useful to himself, and a great comfort to his mother, whose blind love vailed her eyes to many of his deficiencies.

The Log School House seemed to have an inspiring genius perched in its rafters, for study was the rule and not the exception among the new and old pupils, and the master was very, very happy. Rhetorical exercises were introduced with not a little shyness on the part of the performers, but still with unexpected success.

A materialist would, without doubt, ascribe all this enthusiasm to the weather and the health of the students, but there was a more potent influence than atmospheric or physical power could produce.

There came to them in the beginning of winter a

teacher of spiritual truths, to speak to them with the utterance of inspiration, brought out of the Book of all other books, and the few who listened were captive to its control.

Those first Sundays of religious service were strangely mingled with pathos and absurdity. Men and women, whose biblical instruction had been legendary, except as they drew it directly from the fountain-head, the precious Book itself, looked with curiosity upon the man who had come among them, to teach them the Way of Life, and older people wiped misty eyes for the sake of dear memory. Children, sunburned and eager, with the inquisitiveness of young years unanswered, and what was harder for them, indefinite and wordless, but still clamorous in their tangled thoughts for reply, stood with "graceful ankles, bare and brown," agape before their elders, peering unwinkingly into the face of the spiritual speaker, whose countenance was beautiful with the thoughts he brought them, drawn from the text: *If any man love not the Lord Jesus Christ, let him be anathema maranatha.*

This was like Alchemy, separating the people into two distinct divisions, the one led by the young minister who occupied the Log School House on the Sabbath days, and the other by the distiller with the horse-mill.

There was a fierce struggle, and for years, during which time there was little abatement, when worldly necessity did not crowd too closely upon them, to hush for a little the contest. The hydra-head, however, was never wholly conquered, and never will be, till the Millennium. So bitter were the enemies of the truth that there were few, even of the good, who could by any possibility of faith or imagination become Chiliasts.

John Haxton became one of the chief supporters of the church party. How the good Father led him to this path, is only known to himself. Whether it was the failure of his broad acres to satisfy, or the disappointment he received through his pride and love for his wayward son, or the growing discomfort of his home, no one will ever know; but the sweet peace of believing made his rough, hard face softer, his voice lower and sweeter; and his affection for the far-off boy, who came to him over the graves of a household, deepened, and became stronger and purer.

About the beginning of winter, when the cold seemed to have taken all unawares, and gotten a firmer grip at the tender, quivering flesh of every one; when the snow had made its advent unexpectedly, and found no preparation for it, a solemn warning fell upon the distiller's party.

Abel Winthrop had gone to the mill one afternoon, and when the night came down upon the family, there was a deep sadness, an unutterable dread over each one, as there ever was when he went to that place. Good, generous, noble, and tender as he always was, when the fiend of the cup did not possess him, he was changed horribly on those days, or rather nights, when he came from the mill. The dear little ones shuddered, and crept off to bed with no supper, and only a long, close, sobbing hug from mother, and a kiss from Robert—a long clinging kiss, such as comes from burdened breasts—and they huddled closely under the covers, and with unspoken dread, and arms clasped, said their simple prayers, the same their mother used to say when a child, and which the loving Father never wearies of hearing, and fell asleep. Oh, sleep, sleep! Blessed are they whose sorrows and fears are not too heavy for slumber!

On this early winter night, the winds were ferocious in their revels, snatching at the small windows, clutching at the loose boards, and roaring down the throats of the great stone-chimneys, whistling a wild, unearthly melody under the eaves, and moaning beneath the ill-fitted doors of the farm-house unceasingly. The hours waned slowly as mother and son, with the settee drawn up before the fitful blaze, sat with arms about each other in silence, waiting, waiting, waiting! Oh, the bitter pain of such watching! The agony of such anxious vigils! By-and-by the clock's slow, monotonous voice tolled the hour of midnight, and yet no sound came, save the cry of the storm. Mrs. Winthrop rose, with slow and determined step and gesture, folded herself in her blanket, and wrapping her boy in another, said, "Robert, he is my husband, and I love him with all his faults; and he is your father. Let us go for him." Both forgot the many miserable hours he had brought them, the disgrace that lay upon a drunkard's wife and boy, and faced the storm with as much eagerness as if he were their ideal of love, goodness, and purity. All was forgotten even before they met the panting horses trudging through the snow alone, guided only by that strange thing men have named instinct. This indication gave them supernatural strength, and they hurried on and on, where there were no houses, no tracks even of the wagon they had passed, so busy was the storm in hiding every path of man. Through the drifted whiteness, hand in hand they went, breasting the storm, unheeding the howling of that angry night, only listening now and then for the voice they feared would call to them no more, only in remembrance.

Nothing came to their aching ears, and exhaustion was hindering their weary footsteps somewhat, when Mrs. Winthrop fell forward across some obstruction that caught her flying feet. That same strange teaching that took the poor shivering horses to their home, told her in a moment what she touched, and with an almost or quite superhuman strength,—for such love as led her to him through the midnight and its beating storm, is not of earth,—she lifted up his white, still face, and the hurrying clouds made a parting for the moonlight to fall upon the hushed lips, and she saw that he still breathed. She thanked God with more fervency than she had ever prayed, as she felt the throbbing of his heart under his unfastened coat. Mother and son bore the heavy man over the small snow mountains, now and then stopping to regain their exhausted strength, and chafe the benumbed hands and feet of the sleeper, who but for the bravery of love, would never have awakened to this life any more. Home at last, they laid him upon the settee, where the two had waited and counted the hours, and with an energy that necessity always brings, strove to restore him again to consciousness. The gray daylight, and the lull of the storm found him writhing in pain, and delirious with fever, but there was life and hope, and the wife was almost happy. Three of his fingers were frozen, and but for the greater pain he had felt at his heart, he would have moaned aloud. This was nothing. Weeks were counted to him on a bed of pain, and from a distant town came a surgeon to save if possible a part of the hand that had once dealt so tenderly and heroically with his loved ones at home. This was sorrow unutterable to the husband, who knew why and how the pain came to himself, and to her he loved, and he sacredly pledged himself anew to be loving, gentle, and watchful for her happiness evermore. He was her Nemesis, and meant to be true and good, but ah me!

Robert was so happy when they were all well again, and his father went to the mill and came back unconquered. With a child's faith he thought the sorrows of his young life all past, and the future looked fair and glad to him.

Beautiful, hopeful boyhood!

## CHAPTER VII.

"Oh, enviable, early days,
  When dancing thoughtless pleasure's maze,
To care, to guilt unknown!
How ill exchanged for riper times,
To feel the follies, or the crimes,
  Of others, or my own!"

It was a sermon to all who went to the distillery, and even the distiller was careful not to permit too much whisky to be drank in cold weather. He had grown rich on his traffic with souls. Now he commenced throwing new chains around his victims. He had money. He had money to lend, and many an ambitious young man thought the shrewd financier growing generous and kindly, because he would spare it; but never thought that the mortgage given would not expire till the land would double in value by the increasing demand for it, and perhaps something of misfortune or miscalculation would throw it into his grasping hands. And so they were encouraged to purchase with no capital of their own, and the possession of the distiller's money made them careful to keep friends with him, which in this place of limited, emotional vernacular, found expression in a glass of grog. Few escaped without a desperate struggle with themselves and the distiller, and many, ah! so many fell.

This wonderful escape from death served as a theme of many a Temperance Lecture in the Log School House. Nelson Winthrop was too tenderly touched by the event to speak of it to his pupils; but his pale, sad face was eloquent, and they carried the remembrance of it for days, wherever they went.

Even Peter Dally knew what it meant, this horrible event, and when he went into his teacher's house the night after, he took his great shoes off in the door-way, and entered softly and with instinctive reverence. He seemed to understand that there had been a second dawning in his life, and that Mr. Winthrop had touched the sealed fountain of thought, and he loved him almost to idolatry. No sacrifice was too great, and when the coldest mornings dawned in the winter, master Winthrop found huge embers and luxuriant warmth about the hearth of his school-room, when he entered, and to his utter amazement, by constant early watching for his unknown friend, he saw the uncouth figure of Peter crouching and stooping along under the fences to escape unobserved from his kindly deed. Of course no recognition could be made of the thoughtful affection, but a clearer and more comprehensive course of education was decided upon for the lad. His soul escaped so slowly from its imprisonment, that he could not be taught much that way, and so his bungling hands were instructed to use the ax and plane. Hewing was so needed in that region that he could very well get a comfortable income at such employment, and he was delighted with his first lessons.

Sandy was getting on wonderfully. The strides he

took in his Latin and the quick insight into Greek, were almost miraculous. The brain was in working order at last, and it would speed past those which were of lighter calibre and quicker in the primary motions. He had a great heart, and it beat with the best and truest throb of a loving nature. There was nothing too grand for him to achieve, and he laid all his positive and probable acquirements at the feet of his teacher, as her success and not his own. He almost deified the girl in his admiration and adoration of her goodness and mental possessions.

Charlie Haxton was hurrying downward with that strange speed that sin gives to the feet of its votaries. Already the glow of youth was changed to the fevered flush of the wine. His father's remonstrance was of no avail, and his mother's querulous lectures—she had forgotten any other style of communication—made him worse, and he reveled his life and strength away.

Benjamin had written home but once during the winter, and then there was a package of letters, sent by a chance traveler, for letters were a luxury in those days, in which but comparatively few indulged. They were an era in the lives of the receivers, and preserved as precious possessions to be lent and carefully returned to the happy owners.

Even Rollin began to his friends, except the one to Mary, with :—

"MY DEAR FRIEND :—I take my pen in hand to inform you that I am well, and hope these few lines will find you enjoying the same blessing, etc., etc." The remainder was in the stiff, awkward style that non-usage gives to such communications. Mostly on health, the weather, the prices of produce, and politics. Not so, his letter to Mary, though there was not one word, or hint of what the future might be to them, it was descriptions of the outer world, and the splendid schemes of great men, and the benevolent projects of the good and God fearing. Something of his progress, the books he had read, the church where he listened to great truths, and the hope that the world would be no worse for his existence, and closed by saying however much the winter had been to him, the *spring* was welcome.

She knew what that spring meant. It was enough, and this much even she needed. O, how fair the days looked to be with that letter, wrapped to spare the neatness of its folding, and hidden away in—where girls carry letters from those they love best!

Annette Gordon made her appearance the next summer as the teacher in the Log School House! This was astonishing and quite unsatisfactory to all parties except the Gordon family. But she felt the dignity of her family at stake, and quite won upon the people by her efforts to please. In striving to be faithful to others, she bettered herself.

The Haxton family were astonished when the spring added to their family, a daughter-in-law, introduced as Mrs. Priscilla Allen Haxton.

For the benefit of the feminine readers it must be recorded how the bride was dressed. A bonnet of domestic manufacture, which a confused memory of something seen sometime by Mrs. Allen in her younger days, concocted of a gayly tinted small shawl, and burdened with the remnants of antiquated artificial blossoms, which never imitated any thing, and might with no irreverence be worshiped, as they were in the likeness of nothing in the earth beneath, and surely, according to our ideas of heaven, could not be found there. Her dress was of cotton, whose bleaching process had been interrupted very prematurely, and had been gotten up in habitable form in an incredibly short space of time. The only articles which had been added to the external portion of her costume, were a pair of green morocco shoes, a white lace vail, and a pair of pink-cotton gloves. She seemed to have ignored drapery, for, cold as was the spring morning, when she made her advent, there was nothing to shield her from the damp winds. Charlie Haxton had taken this poor, half-witted girl, not for love—he could truly love no one—but partly because he did not know what he did, and partly with a dim idea of punishing his family for calling to his mind Benjamin Rollin as an example of all goodness. Poor girl! It was a sore fall for all your fancies, this first reception into the richest family of all the Ridge.

God help you!

She had a sort of love for her husband—a peculiar kind, it was made up of craving for money and what it could bring, partly of gratitude, for he was the first and only young man who had noticed her, and partly of that unreasonableness which causes half the women to love till death, the men who ask them to.

The household storm was stilled by the philosophy and determination of its head, who seldom interfered in its smaller turmoil; but this was a serious matter, and involved more than he wished to risk, and he assumed the guardianship of the new daughter and defended her from the tongued onslaughts of the two feminine members of the house of Haxton. While the son was sullen and silent, a few words of undoubted authority settled all appearance of disturbance, but left the poor bride of a day to the petty torments of a lifetime.

The coming of Benny Rollin was the signal of better nature outwardly on the part of Miss Araminta, and but for this lull in the domestic turmoil, the young wife would have wept her eyes blind. She tried, poor thing! to be good and pleasant, and her absurd attempts at being agreeable were worse than any thing else for them to endure.

Benjamin had taken on the polish of a gentleman, and had that air which a refined nature gets so soon from contact with its kind. Not that this is needed exactly to make a true man, but those graceful acts of politeness, those delicate amenities of cultivated life, carry a wonderful amount of influence with them, and Benjamin had felt the need of them when he first emerged from his backwoods life, but without positive attention, unconsciously adopted them. To Mary Winthrop, whose two hands were held out to him in greeting, he was the same noble and true friend, and she stilled her heart and steadied her voice to say:—

"I am very glad, Benny, so happy to hear your voice once more," and he looked down into her saintly soul through her quiet, steadfast eyes, and said nothing for the choking that hindered his speech, and great round tears gathered and fell upon the hand he held, and he turned to Mrs. Winthrop, dear motherly Mrs. Winthrop, and to the beloved teacher, with warm greeting. Mary went outside the little "spare room," that she might lift that hand made sacred now, unseen, to her lips, and coming presently sat silent listening to the conversation, and to the casual observer seemed as if she were only a hearer, because she must be; but the deepening of the dark of her soft eyes, the pressure of the exquisite lips against her two rims of pearls, and now and then a caressing attention to that hand on which the tear fell, revealed more than she had even whispered to herself in the stillness of her chamber. Oh, but she asked nothing more of life than it gave her now! Her cup was brimmed with happiness and jeweled with hope! It was to her believing nature tangible enough, and she did not strive to unwind the tangled threads that glistened in the future, waiting only for fate to unite the web and woof of their two lives with the ceaseless shuttle of time. As in a dream it all came to her, and she believed as if it were a real and sacred revelation.

All were happy in his return, save perhaps John Haxton, who felt a two-fold emotion when he took the hand of the boy and bade him welcome. One was of sincere gladness and intense satisfaction, and the other the faded hope of his own first-born, the one who lay in his great broad bosom a little tender helpless thing, and made the first soft nestling place it had ever carried.

But he tugged at his hope for this one, and tried to escape with it into the future, leaving the past and present with its burden of sorrows. He was so strangely softened, that Rollin was amazed, until when the evening had waned, he called "Silly" to "fetch the Bible and let Benny read a verse or two, as his eyes were somehow bad that night." And "Silly" was only too happy to perform any service for her only friend in the household. Charlie was home that night, and it was a remarkable event, that it should happen so, but for

Benny's sake they thought, and it was, as they supposed. Through kindly feeling, when Benny had read the Fifty-First Psalm, and lifted up his eyes from the sweet singer's plaintive notes, his gaze fell upon the dark, fierce eyes of Charles Haxton, and from that look he measured the hatred of his boyhood's companion. He knew then that if the future held any sorrow for him that did not come direct from the All-loving, it would be dealt by the hand of this votary of the distiller. He knew Charlie was and always had been envious, bitterly so, but he was cowardly, and whatever he did to an enemy was in the dark, always. To be careful, to be obliging, and to forbear noticing his mood, was the intent of Rollin, and for the sake of the father who looked so broken, to avoid even by endurance any rupture between them. He treated "Silly" with the same unaffected kindness and respect that he gave to the other members of the family, which more than any thing served to allay the storm for a little. She, poor soul! was fascinated by the charm of his manner, and like a true descendant of "La belle France," adapted his deportment to her own use with singular variations, to the amusement of her new father, and to the anger and disgust of her husband. Patient Benny did not quite like to be caricatured, even though the most reverential of friends performed the principal parts, with the intensest admiration for her inspiration in her new *role*. Poor "Silly!" she bore her husband's neglect and his harshness with not a word of retort or expostulation, and only that her sleeve or the corner of her apron did duty for her wet eyes, no one would have known that she felt her position. But she grew thin and pale, and when the hard duties of the farmer's household were performed, she went away alone as if solitude and silence were the only friends. A word of kindness from her husband, or a trifling gift, would lift her changeable spirits into a state of extatic delight. The summer wore away, and Benny studied the books the professors had recommended to him, and a skeleton loaned him by the old doctor, who had long since ceased to wonder at its marvelous mechanism, amid the dulling routine of his sluggish life. This last he kept hidden away, and only with bolted door, ventured an examination of this once soul animated frame work. Had any one save Mr. Haxton discovered this new inmate in the house, there would have been troublous times with the young seeker after strange truths. People unaccustomed to biology have a natural antipathy for human bones, which changes to reverent admiration, with the study of their structure. This should be taught children very early, but it was not ventured upon at this time, even by Nelson Winthrop, who dared do almost any thing that was right, but the steps of progress are slow, and he felt that the time for such mysteries had not yet dawned upon the Log School House.

## CHAPTER VIII.

"How blessed are the beautiful!
  Love watches o'er their birth;
O beauty! in my nursery
  I learned to know thy worth;
For even there I often felt
  Forsaken and forlorn;
And wished—for others wished it, too—
  I never had been born."

ANNETTE GORDON taught only as she had learned the art from the various instructors who had swayed the scepter in the Log House. She was orderly, prompt, and diligent. She exacted the most prompt and perfect obedience from her pupils,—a lesson she had learned at home where parental rule was autocratic. She did not soften the little hearts of the children by the ugly ferule with which she used to harden their small hands. This was the only mode of punishment of which she had any knowledge, except stooping to point to a crack in the floor for a half hour, or holding a stone in the hand with the muscles firm and straight. These last were too time-consuming, and she preferred the first as expeditious and effectual. She had mingling with her virtues and failings, a love of pretty things, and she taught what she had never learned herself, namely, drawing.

One pencil had to accomplish it all, but very pretty pictures came from the hand of this young *dilettante* in art, and also from her pupils. It served to spare for that summer, the few bare spots on the walls for future pilgrims to this temple of wisdom, and gave them a rude and imperfect idea of the pleasure of transferring to one's possession, a tangible shape of the scenes which have met the eyes. It was meager, but it was a dawning, and the afterward of many of their lives took a smile from the remembrance of this first lesson in fine arts.

So the summer waned with its blossoms and fruitage, as summers had done before, with but few mile stones for memory, and but few headlands passed in the voyage of life, whose shapes could be remembered by the many who dwelt on the Ridge. When the autumn came again fully, and the preparation for Benny's departure made busy hands in the farm-house of the Haxtons, that heavy glare of anger rested once more upon the recipient of so much care and attention, from the eyes of the heir of the predial property. In the summer days when the hay was being mown, or the grain being gathered, with an appearance of equality between them, the old hatred was in a measure forgotten, and Rollin had even got so far on in friendship, as to remonstrate with the reckless fellow, and receive kindly assurances of a better life, and the student offered a word, too, of expostulation for the sake of the simple-hearted creature Charlie had taken to his home; and this had roused no anger, and proved the acceptance of the reproof, by a pleasanter greeting to the falling creature who had been the sport of his fearful career. But now he was torturing in his treatment of the girl whenever his father's ear was too much occupied to observe his words, and Rollin was present to endure it with her through his exquisite sympathies. John Haxton would have offered his son a separate maintenance, as became a rich man to do, but that he feared the young wife would die of neglect.

With this anger burning in the veins of Charlie, Benny parted from them all, carrying the memory of many a sweet hour with Mary, and the hope of a lifetime by her side, though not a word of all this had passed from lip to lip,—yet by the cunning intercommunication of kindred thoughts, which had pulsed through the silence, each comprehended the other and was content,—nay, more than that, *satisfied*.

That last word is the most comprehensive in the language. Happiness may have its alloy, but to be satisfied is better than to be glad. It implies the peace—the rest—the balm of the soul; and these two young travelers felt it in the full depths of their beings.

And so the winter came between them.

It was a winter brimmed with toil, made easy by hope. Mary had assisted her father not a little in the schoolroom, for his painful weakness was unusually troublesome, and sometimes he was absent altogether, and the smaller tax-payers grumbled in a half-suppressed way at his absence from the post where he received their petty amount of money. That Mary assisted him gratuitously even when he was on full duty, they never took into account. Such a man as Winthrop never performs less than his duty. True, he was employed for six hours, but they oftener stretched themselves to eight, with stupid pupils, or absentees who had returned and desired to be even with their classes, and a seeker for knowledge could not be denied, no matter what the effort cost the master. Robert Winthrop was a great comfort to him, and his own boy, droll little Ellis, was crawling hard after his sister in the big Lexicons with Sandy McLain. Some of his first year's pupils were already off in the large towns, learning life in its other phases, and getting the good of the instruction received in the Log School House. Many were the inaudible blessings which were uttered for the good man, but his own house praised and blessed him more than any. His brother, with the ruined hand ever before him, restrained his taste for the fiery cup, and the glad family learned to look upon the father's half helplessness as a blessing. But there were others who had forgotten; and the young pastor's remonstrance, nor sweet home-love, nor ties of affection could hold them from the fascination of the arch enemy, and some fell in the bloom of their young years. God pity them —and pity more, those who are left!

About this time a happy thought struck John Haxton. He would build a mill by the creek, far off from the distillery, and then there would be less excuse for visiting the delusive place, and with the suggestive thought came the future mill up before his mind, and its blessings like magic, and almost as soon, rose the mill and all the belongings. Before the "Lazy Man," as this summer's master was called, had dragged out the first week of his term, the sound of the grinders was heard from the school-room windows, and mingled with the buzz of whisperers. Rollin expected to remain after the winter's course was completed for private tuition; and the snowy days somehow did not seem quite welcome to Mary, but

"It was a bitter cold, blustery day in winter, when the tidy sleigh of John Haxton came for Mary." Page 75.

she hurried in and out of the house like a young bird, and brought the sunshine with her whenever she came.

It was a bitter cold, blustery day in winter, when the tidy sleigh of John Haxton came for Mary, at the request of Mrs. Charlie, as they called the young wife. She had been "broken," so the rough messenger said, and wanted to see Miss Mary; with a fearful foreboding of what might have prompted the call, she rode in silence to the doorway, in which stood the slouched figure of Charlie—silent and remorseful, unable to lift his eyes to the pure face of the young girl, and only saying, "Glad you've come. It's only a notion of the girl, and father would humor her."

Mary entered the chamber where the pale, crushed creature lay, and saw in her loosely folded arms a dead babe, which she would not relinquish, and now and then kissed with a mute tenderness that held in its appeal sufficient pathos to soften any heart under a human form.

"Oh, Mary, thank you. I'm going with my baby, but I don't just know how to part with Charlie. It was so good of him to marry me who ain't like other folks, nor was my mother afore me, but father loved her always." Here she sighed, and seemed to be away in memory. By-and-by, returning to her thoughts, she said, "Do you think he'll care because I took baby with me? I couldn't help it. Won't you tell him so for me, Mary? He'll may-be believe you. Do you think he will be angry if I ask to see him? I—I want, oh! so much to see mother, oh! so much. Please call him quick!" and when Miss Haxton came back with the young husband, the white peace of death had drifted over her face, and the sparkle of her eyes exceeded any flash they ever wore in life, and she seemed almost radiant by that strange phenomenon which sometimes comes to illume the dark valley.

The young husband was awed and softened by the sight of this wreck, ebbing out into the dark sea that knows no boundary, and stooping over the passing wife, said, as if the words were wrung from him:—

"I'm sorry, my girl. I wish I had been kinder to you." And the face, radiant before, lit up with a perfect glory of supreme happiness, as she heard these parting words, and then the shadow fell, dull, gray, and ashen, over her face, and she was gone.

They parted the last lingering snows in the graveyard to make a resting spot for the young wife and mother, and the innocent babe whom the good Father had called in mercy to himself. It was sad to hear the sobbing of poor Mrs. Allen over her child when the young man turned from his wife and babe; it was as if he were given over by the grieved spirit of God to the fate he had chosen, and thereafter there would be no obstacle in his way to utter ruin.

Guy Foster, the young apostle in the wilderness, in vain tried to take his hand and lead him away from the destiny beckoning to him, and the syren voices calling to him from the bewildering depths of the fatal wineglass. His heart was steeled, perhaps with remorse—who can tell?

And he gave it to the keeping of fiends henceforth.

His grieved father touched his head with his trembling palm in an almost unbelievable tenderness, so hard and rough had his expressions always been, and begged him to come home as a little child, and live for the hope and happiness of those who loved him still, and for the good of his own soul; but the boy—for he was nothing more—wrung himself from his father's grasp, and the struggle was for ever past. He had sown the wind, and must reap the whirlwind; but poor "Silly" had gathered her harvest of tares and tears, and was at last freed from "the fitful fever, and slept well." Peace to her soul!

Mrs. Haxton was sorry, even tearful, for in natures like hers pity is stronger than love, and regret more potent than forbearance. It had been like an evil dream to the household, whose awakening was sorrowful by the vivid remembrance. And the shadow lay sullen and immovable, till Benjamin Rollin came back and brought a different element into their domestic crucible, making a new compound entirely. As the sunbeam is said to warp the strongest tower, so did the light of his presence turn the faces of the Haxton family toward the warm glow of a better life. Goodness of the heart is powerful in whatever strange element it mingles, and to make the waters of Marah sweet seemed his mission to that family.

Time strews blossoms to hide even the graves where the bitterest tears fall, and it did not take many flowers to cover this new mound from the thoughts of those from whose circle she faded into the silent land. Many hoard their grief for the dead, and almost feast upon their sorrow, as if there were tastes and touches of sweetness in their very sadness, and sometimes,

"Will the soul
Snatch the first moment of forgetfulness
To wander like a restless child away."

So it was with the Haxtons. Benjamin, the new mill, and the summer's hopes and labors, crowded the girl quite into the past, and the mound had not greened in the spring rain before her name roused no echo in the house where for a single brief year she had tarried. Only her mother, who had not been called in time to get one parting word or smile, remembered and wept over her fate in the loneliness and desolation of her old age.

John Haxton felt this omission, and in his awkward but efficient way showed his sympathy by many a generous expression.

## CHAPTER IX.

"Dim, backward as I cast my view,
  What sickening scenes appear!
What sorrows yet may pierce me through
  Too justly I may fear!
    Still caring, despairing,
      Must be my bitter doom;
    My woes here shall close ne'er
      But with the closing tomb!

THE "Lazy Man" half dozed away the summer hours, letting the children perform such gymnastic feats in and about the school-room as would delight an admirer of acrobats, or a modern cultivator of infantile muscle. When the directors visited the institution there was a display, and the following is a specimen of the entertainment:—

"Jim Gordon, where's the equinoctial line?"

"The twentieth of September and the twentieth of March, most genr'ly speakin'. Sometimes its a little *airlier*, and sometimes not so quick."

"What is the difference between latitude and longitude?"

"Why, sir, one's a black mark stretched around one way, and the 'tother's a black mark stretched around 'tother way."

"What are the poles?"

"They are the spots furdest north and south, when the round part is kind o' peaked or bulged out a little. Nobody hasn't been there to find out jist how 'tis."

"How many days in a year?—the next boy."

"Three hundred and sixty-five days and some odd hours and minutes and seconds."

"What is done with the odd hours, &c?"

"When there's enough of 'em they are hitched together and make a hull day that's jined onto some of the years."

"What is that year called?"

"Bissextile, but it ought to be called *bi-four-tile*, 'cause there's odd bits enough to make a hull one wonct in four year, instead of six."

"What is the shape of the earth?"

"Round."

"How do we move on its surface?"

"Like a fly crawlen round a apple, only he goes on six legs, an' we jist go on two."

"What kind of government have we?"

"Republikin."

"What kind is that?"

"A kind where everybody kin be president, or governor, or justice of the peace, or constable, or any thing he's a mind to, and everybody that's twenty-one, 'cept women, can go to 'lections and vote, and have an all killen good time."

"That last part of your lesson was not *learned* you, sir; you must not add to your answers any remarks of your own. The class may take their benches."

## THE OLD LOG SCHOOL HOUSE.

An amusing incident occurred during the reign of this same master :

> "A great, green, bashful simpleton,
> The butt of all good-natured fun,"

was called up to recite. He had learned his alphabet, and was merging into words of three letters; but he could not comprehend the philosophy of pronouncing. The author of his little cut-off-cut cornered book, that the lesson might be easy for beginners, had classified words of similar terminations and sounds in groups, a method common at that day, but justly rejected now. On this occasion, our blundering hero, was called up to repeat his lesson, and after scratching his unkempt head, and twisting his face into divers apologetic expressions, preparatory to the great effort before him, he commenced with a snapping-turtle tone, cutting off each letter by itself, lest they might get mixed into a word, thus :—

"H-u-g," and stopped.

"Well, go on David," said the teacher.

"H-u-g."

"Pronounce it."

"*H-u-g,*" repeated the lad with a loud, distinct emphasis on each letter.

"Pronounce it, I say."

"H-U-G," again repeated David, utterly at a loss to know what more *could* be required.

"*Pronounce it,*" again vociferated the teacher, in a half angry tone.

Then with all the force of a healthy arrangement of lungs, David once more roared,

"H-U-G."

This was too much for the teacher to endure, so giving David a rap over the knuckles with the ferule, he thought he would aid him a little in the difficulty, and spelt the word for him:—

"H-u-g, spells hug. Now go on, and be smart."

David now imagined he had the key-note that would unlock the whole column of *sound*, and rattled off in double quick time,

"H-u-g, *hug*, t-u-g, *hug*, r-u-g, *hug*, m-u-g, *hug*—"

"Stop, stop," cried the teacher, "*they are not all hugs*, you blockhead."

Poor David! He has made slow progress in learning. He can not read nor write, and is now a forsaken old bachelor. That hugging scrape vanquished him!

These were perhaps as ludicrous as any part of the series of oral instructions he had in his wakeful and energetic moments given them, but extremes always suggest proper mediums, and contemplators of these retrospective scenes, may, if they can, imagine many useful lessons learned that summer in the Log School House. This man "boarded round," and when the week came for him to stop with Nelson Winthrop, albeit he did not patronize the school, he presented a little fine cupboard to Mrs. McLain, in consideration of what he would eat and sleep at her house, for those seven allotted days, and thus escaped the infliction of the "Lazy Man's" society.

It was before the harvest days that Benjamin Rollin had returned. He was just a trifle pale with too close application to his books, and a lack of that activity which had made up the most of his life; and Mary's face whitened too, when she saw him, but an explanation soon stilled the strange throbbing of fear at her young heart, and the gladness she had waited for so patiently, filled her sweet soul like an overflowing goblet of Nepenthe. All were glad to have him back save Charlie; but his heart would never be truly glad for any thing any more. The new mill was given to the wayward son as an offering of peace and repentance for any earlier wrongs; but he neglected it and a man was hired to care for it. Nelson Winthrop had endeavored with that delicate tact which tender natures always possess, to lead him back to happiness, but alas! it was too late—too late!

The young man's hatred for his adopted brother seemed to the recipient of his malice to have grown tenfold more bitter, and yet there was less outward manifestation of it than usual. He permitted Rollin to describe life and people abroad, without interpolating with a single sneer, as after the first winter in Philadelphia. His interest, and the words which manifested it, seemed genuine to all save the narrator, who felt, by that persuasion for which we can give no reason, that it was only lip-deep, or buried from casual eyes, by some fearful meaning. This appearance, with an unusual meaning of speech, was related in confidence to Nelson Winthrop, who only replied, by saying it was a trifle of envy.

About this time a fearful accident occurred very near the Log School House. Peter Dally was hewing lumber in the woods which stretched backward from the house where the children chased the fitful shadows in the summer time; and his mother, grown proud and tender of him, and craving a sight and sound of her boy, went to carry him a mid-day lunch, and was crushed by a falling tree. It seemed as if the tree had grown for hundreds of years, and waited there to fulfil a destiny which involved so much of this world's mystery. This world's mystery! When the vail is rent it will all seem simple, and wisely and lovingly ordered; but the blow fell with more pain upon the heart of poor Peter, than it did upon the quivering mass which the boy found, when the cry of fear from the upturned face of the woman reached him. John Haxton was at the mill, and at the wild call from the woods, first reached the still conscious woman and her smitten son.

"Be good to my boy; tell them to be kind to my poor child," was all she had strength to utter, and the pain ceased and her weary life was done.

"I will! so help me God," solemnly answered the man of few words; and be it here recorded, he kept in spirit and in deed, to the full, his vow over the dead that summer day. And so Guy Foster performed again the burial service in the Log School House, and enjoyed the blessed privilege of speaking of peace and joy for the sorrowing, and of a resurrection and never ending intercourse with the beloved hereafter. Peter comprehended all this. The human in his nature was fully developed by this last shock. Like the effect of electric currents upon benumbed people, so had sorrow and fear thrilled the dormant soul of the boy, and expanded it, fold after fold, and though it would never flutter away with the wings of fancy, or be borne upward by imagination to the realms of poesy, yet he would have what was better than genius and all these joy or tear-bringing gifts—a good, believing soul—a faithful, loving heart. Sorrow is the cross that lifts many a one heavenward, and opens Paradise to countless mortals. Many there are, too, who would never have sailed into the haven of rest at last, if only the silvery crested waves of prosperity had circled the prow of their life-boat. Storms have driven them to a sure anchor. The poor fellow watched and tended her grave, for it was all there was left to him, as the father slept years ago, and he was taken home with a strange tenderness to the house of John Haxton. He was useful, and it roused no ire in the bosom of his son that this poor fellow chanced to be there. In truth, he seemed absorbed in other matters, and paid little or no heed to the new-comer. Peter was overwhelmed with the kindness of Mr. Haxton, the rich man, who had never even noticed him, much less spoken a pleasant word to him. He would have done any thing henceforth to give him happiness or spare him pain. It seemed as if the love of a woman had nested itself in his great heart, and he had poured it over the common-place and rather unlovely life of his benefactor and friend. It amounted to servility, which, had it been bestowed upon a wicked man, would have made a villain's tool of him, with his narrow range of thought and unenlightened conscience. Even Mary Winthrop was shrined in memory, to be no part of his future life, only as a lovely dream that returns to our thoughts, or like a half-forgotten hymn—a snatch of old-time melody would she be to him thereafter. Sometimes when Mr. Haxton was absent making sales for his grain and wool, the poor lad would wander off in his loneliness to that new grave, and moan away the evening; and sometimes, unable to count the hours, the dark night wrapped him in his foldings; but with instinctive knowledge he found his way home, and with a footfall like a cat, reached in safety his little silent chamber in the loft over the kitchen fire. People in such simple communities scarcely know the use of bolt or lock to their habitations, and some would even fear to turn them, from superstitious awe of shutting out some spectral good. So Peter's ways were unnoticed, save that Benjamin had seen him once creeping home in the moonlight from his dead mother.

One morning he seemed strangely affected, unable to attend to his duties, quite incoherent in his usually not too distinct style of conversation, and Mrs. Haxton, unused yet to his moods, supposed this was a part of his strangeness and took little heed of him; but on the return of his new friend, he rushed up to him, and clasping his long, uncouth hands, exclaimed, "O, sir, O, sir, I don't know any thing, I couldn't know any thing; please don't ask me if I do," and then fell into a torpid condition, from which he wakened only after days and days of illness, in which he raved for his mother, and said she was taken away, which surprised no one, so recent had been her death, and knowing that she was all the world to him.

It was the Sabbath after the poor lad's attack, that with the utmost consternation it was announced that Mrs. Dally's grave was empty! The coffin lay upon the top of the grave, and her remains were not to be found. No one who has never mingled with such uncultivated people, can imagine the horror they felt; and blended with their wild fancies, was the natural antipathy which every one feels at such a desecration.

Some had heard noises; others had seen lights; one had been visited with a strange and foreboding vision; a looking-glass had been broken; three raps had been distinctly counted out upon some one's head-board; the closed doors of some house had all been found open in the morning; the milk had all turned sour; the dogs had howled; the cats looked with blood-red eyes; and last of all, some one of veracity, and not a spark of imagination, had seen a stooping figure crawling along in the graveyard after dark, but did not speak of it, because he would be laughed at, or frighten the children. Benjamin Rollin proposed a search. He felt outraged for the sake of the sick boy at home, who he knew if roused from the fever in which he called her name constantly, and found no grave, even, of her left to him, would go wild with grief. And so with a zeal that was wonderful to the excited people, he caught at every clue that would unravel the mystery. When others had wearied out with the excitement, tired of hearing it spoken of even, he was still on the alert. His persistency of character would not permit him to give it up. Had they lived in the vicinity of a Medical School, he would have conjectured how and when and why it was gone; but nothing could by any possibility have occurred like that to poor Mrs. Dally. It must have been wantonness and that alone which disturbed her quiet sleeping. So the days dragged themselves into weeks, and Peter's fever had burned itself out in his hardy nature, and he was slowly coming back to himself again, though there were times of strangeness, which all ascribed to his individual peculiarities, and his disturbed brain. He feared to have Mr. Haxton enter his room, but as for Charlie, he never was troubled with a visit from him. Benjamin had administered to him, and it was considered a miracle that he was restored. The neighbors extolled the young Æsculapius to the clouds, and almost decided that his settling among them would stretch their time of life far beyond the one allotted by the Scriptures.

Mr. Haxton had a double delight in the success, for it saved one *protegé*, and also proved the wisdom of his benevolence in educating the other. But a deep darkness fell upon them. A letter was found written to some unknown person in the highway very near the School House, unfolded, and as if it did not precisely please the writer, he had scrawled it over and cast it aside. It was signed by Benjamin Rollin. It stated that a woman had been killed by an accident, and was therefore an excellent subject for dissection. The body had been exhumed, covered with lime and packed in a barrel, and was hidden under a pile of grain in the yard of John Haxton. The directions were precise, and said any moonless night would do to remove it to a certain place understood, as all curiosity had died away, and no one would be suspicious of strangers, even if seen in the neighborhood. To be sure, the writing was not in his usual handsome round hand, such as master Winthrop always used and taught in his copies, and all the words were not as he would have compounded them; but the excitement he must have been under at the time of writing would have excused that, if the community had not been too effervescing to notice any such little significances of its falsity. The proof of its truth was that the body was found as described, and about it was a coat owned and worn sometime before by the young medical student. Had a star fallen, the noon-day sun been darkened, or any of the strange things prophesied of the latter days, come upon any of them, they would not have been so fearfully shocked. Benjamin Rollin saw that it was needless to cry out against the evidence, and only Mary Winthrop and John Haxton believed it to be a false accusation. If Mary had her belief, she only spoke it to the sufferer, and Mr. Haxton was mystified and would think nothing at all.

## CHAPTER X.

> "Oh! thou who mournest on thy way,
> With longings for the close of day;
> He walks with thee, that Angel kind,
> And gently whispers, 'Be resigned:
> Bear up, bear on, the end shall tell
> The dear Lord ordereth all things well.'"

NELSON WINTHROP, with his good heart and cool judgment, with his love for science and his infatuation for research, gauged the measure of the temptation, and the possible encouragements and excuses a young man in love with his profession might have for such an opportunity to possess something on which he might experiment, and over which he might at leisure study, came to the conclusion, though tardily and reluctantly, that the young man was guilty. The letter surprised him, and would have raised a doubt if he could think of any one courageous and angry enough to plan and execute such vengeance. But to him the real pain of the affair arose from the duplicity of the young man in leading such a search for the body. He would not be reconciled to the falsehood. His heart ached for Mary, who persisted in pleading with him to doubt, even if he could not wholly disbelieve the appearance of guilt. Benjamin, in his young pride and conscious integrity, would not stoop to deny so base a charge. He knew why it was, and who had conspired to ruin him, and it was very hard to bear. To his foster father he only said:—

"You know I did not do this wrong. You are and have been too kind to me to permit me, even if I was tempted, which I was not, to do any thing to make you regret all you have done for me. But I can not disprove it now, and perhaps never may, but the God you trust will not wholly forsake me. I had hoped to settle here, and perhaps make the people better and wiser for your kindness to me, a fatherless and motherless boy. But now it can not be so. All are against me, and I must find a new home. I do not think it even right for me to remain to be tried for the offence before the courts, for I should be punished for another's offence. If there was the first chance for escape, I would take the risk of a trial, but there is none, not one. I shall go forth to-night with no friend and no home."

"You have a friend, and one that will be one till the grave, Benjamin; but the home, oh, my boy, I fear you must make one for yourself among strangers! You must not go without means to care for your present wants, and you can let me know when you need a father."

Here John Haxton broke quite down. After a moment's time he took his great buckskin wallet from the locked till of an old walnut chest, and counted out a large sum for a farmer, and so isolated an one, to possess, and forced it upon the young man, and with wrung hands and wrung hearts they parted. There was no leave-taking of the family; they believed he had fallen and loathed him, but he went to his old teacher who he knew was too practical and upright to imagine conspiracy or intrigue of any sort—a man who in his unsuspicious nature would have starved in the capacity of a detective, and therefore must believe him guilty. There was a pallor on his handsome face, but his eyes were level and steadfast, though his voice was keyed with the minor tones of sadness, as he asked at the door to see Mary alone. He had never made such a request before, and pity, rather than justice or judgment, made the father ask him to enter the little "spare room," where Mary sat thinking till her eyes were like fire, and her little hands on that summer day, were like the last winter's snow. It was her first grief, and oh! it was bitterer to bear than death. Had she looked into his still white face, she would have known where the reunion would be; but now she could only see a dreary, dreary future, and not one gleam of gladness all the way to their separate graves. She did not dream that it were possible to go to him even without her father's blessing, and she knew Benjamin would not ask it.

Here they stood face to face, alone, as he had desired. She did not hear his changed voice, and as he looked into her startled face, in silence, she rose and giving him her cold hand, said, with a steady tone, in which was concentrated all the heroism of a woman's devotion, when her heart is good and true:—

"Benjamin Rollin, I know you are innocent. There is no voice but your own that can make me believe the sin is yours. As I think now I shall think for ever. Away across years and over graves we *may* see each other again; if not, there is a hereafter where the secret things of this world are revealed."

"Thank God, you do not doubt me! You and my foster father and the One above us, dear Mary, are all who are spared me of my many friends, but these are enough. Some time you will hear from me. Heaven bless you, Mary," and with his two hands resting upon her shoulders, he looked down into her anxious face, while the pale lips answered:—

"May it be so, Benjamin Rollin, may it be so!"

And they parted in tears, amid fondest farewells and dearest hopes of a bright future by-and-by. But the separation was long and desolate to each heart.

It was nearing twilight, and Nelson Winthrop with great sorrow and an expression of forgiveness, which was more painful than accusation itself, parted from his best beloved pupil—the star that had lit the memory of all his ill-requited toils in the Log School House. Sandy McLain followed him as he departed from the place of Mr. Winthrop, and waited for one word. He sprang from his hiding-place, and with the great tears tumbling over his swollen cheeks, exclaimed:—

"Benjie, Benjie, it's na' for me to comfort ye, laddie, but in my heart I ken ye didna do it. I'll be gude to Mary when ye're gangrel. Be cantie, sir, be cantie. Daylight will keek through a sma' hole, I ken. God pity you, Benjie," and with a jerk at the Scotch cap, and a squeeze of the palm, they parted. Somehow this young Scotchman's comfort, though but partly comprehended, lifted his poor sinking heart wonderfully. "Daylight will peep through a small hole, I know," he said, over and over to himself, as he walked past every house whose inmates were familiar to him, and midnight found him on the banks of the quiet Ohio river, and in the morning he was floating down its current upon a raft toward Cincinnati, with no purpose, waiting for Providence to indicate the path he should take. He had his portmanteau and himself to care for, and his disappointed hopes and burden of disgrace to carry into a strange life. It was no easy thing, with his sympathetic nature, to feel alone in the world. It was very hard to look backward to the graves of his household, and to the few who had loved him, and now sorrowed over him as if he were dead. The rough people he had left seemed so good and true, the half-cultivated farm lands lovely, and the plain Old Log School House was the dearest spot now in memory.

When would the shadows be lifted?

He could not believe it would be so always. God loved his children too well to try them beyond their strength. He would part the vail by-and-by, if he trusted Him; and so with hope and courage and the blessing of youth, and its rebounding capabilities, he journeyed on. Not that he was fearful of pursuit; he knew where he was gone no one would follow, but the rumor might, and he wished to build a new character, where there would be no blight to touch it from the past. It was near the Mississippi where he first thought of halting. There was a fearful epidemic raging among the people along the shores of this great river, and providentially entering a low-roofed house where death was brooding with its white wings, he felt that the spirit that directs the believing children, said to him, "Here rest thee—here is thy labor." And he took upon himself his ministry of good. Only a boy he had left home, but years had been counted out to him in the brief time since the shadow fell over his life, and the sign-manual of judgment and faithfulness was written on his face, and

no one shrank from his rule in this reign of terror.
New modes of treatment, such as cleanliness, fresh air,
and sunshine, after the first prescriptions were administered, brought hope to the despairing, and made life
possible, yea, even probable to the heretofore helpless
and hopeless. Had an apostle of good dropped down
from some unknown sphere, there would have been no
more reverence bestowed upon him than was expended
upon the young doctor in the low, miserable village of
Acton. They felt that he was God sent, and when he
saw happiness and comfort springing up at the touch of
his hand, he thought he comprehended the mystery of
Providence, and content came like a dove of peace and
nestled in his heart. He wrote to John Haxton, telling
him of his new home, and bidding him make an opportunity to acquaint Mary of his safety, but not to burden
her with the knowledge of his whereabouts, as questions might trouble her truthful heart. And so it happened.

It was Sunday, after the winter had dropped her
white mantle over the brown leaves and crisped grass,
that Mr. Haxton found Mary walking alone from the
Old Log School House. The young minister had
preached from the text, "*Now ye see as through a glass
darkly,*" and the heavy-hearted girl took courage from
his words, and felt brave to endure her fate.

John Haxton was not a social man, and when he
neared her, and said, "How d'do, Molly?" she felt that
some pleasant thing was in his thoughts. Instinct told
her what it was before he blundered, with his preconceived plan of cautiousness, into the truth. "There's a
doctor alive and well, and doing well, 'way off on the

shore of the biggest river we've got in this country, and he told me—I mean—I—that is,—somebody wrote to me to say so to you. Good day, Molly, I'm almost starved, and the sermon was uncommon long-winded, but jest the thing, Mary, jest the thing. When you want to know any thing mighty bad, come and ask me kind o' sly, you know," and he was off in long strides toward his dinner which he forgot to eat when he got home. And so he fell to dreaming, dreaming—wide-awake dreaming, too, of what at first thought might seem wrong, for it was about worldly things. His son had almost leaped from one ill to another, and now no longer even went to the mill; but wasted his days with the distiller and his whisky. When the horse-mill was of no farther use, remuneratively, and drew no more custom to the distillery, and so with a small amount of management, he had succeeded in having a Post Office established there, the first and only one on the entire Ridge. People who never received a letter oftener than once a year, made frequent visits of inquiry to it; and one would have supposed from the number of visitors, that the government was greatly enriched by this new arrangement.

Charlie Haxton was a daily lounger about it, and very few midnights found him at home. His father had resigned him, as if he were indeed lying cold and still in his coffin, and had he been so laid away, the sorrow might have healed. He was a living trouble to the household.

It was wonderful what pleasure Peter Dally and his strange habits brought to them all. He had learned that tidy boots won the good will of the feminine portion of the family, and he kept them in a remarkable state of cleanliness. But after all he was to them more as a poodle dog is to some lonely woman, or a parrot to one who dislikes stillness, than as a human companion, so greatly had he changed since his illness. Sometimes Guy Foster, who used to talk with him very often, fancied there was a burden upon his mind, which the boy feared might slip off, if he permitted too free conversation, but the shrewdness or simplicity, which ever it might be, baffled the minister. The fellow did not seem to have missed Benjamin, so wholly was he absorbed in his new relations and their interests. And of this poor child did John Haxton think, that Sabbath day afternoon. He must provide for his future support. Not that he remembered his promise over the dying woman, but real interest in the lad, and a growing kindness to every one, fetched the thought. . His money and estates had ceased to give him arrogant airs, or in fact any pleasure of mere possession; and his son would need them but a little time, and his daughter would have use for but a small portion, and he desired to bestow them mostly on Benjamin Rollin, but that would be revealing the young man's whereabouts, and could not be risked. And so he puzzled his brain all that Sabbath afternoon, but the idea came at last, and he found a wonderful appetite for his supper, after such a prolonged fast. He was very indecorous and merry, considering the day, and asked Mrs. Haxton what he should bring from the town, as he started early the next morning,—was sure "Minta" wanted a "bosom-pin with shiny stones in it," and Peter was suffering for a "store cap to wear to meeting." Upon Mrs. Haxton's taking advantage of his mood, and inviting herself to accompany him, his spirits fell, and he was not certain when he would go; and it was too cold anyway for "wimmen folks" to ride so far—and he was off at daylight alone. A will was signed, sealed, and recorded that day, and a wonderful amount of "store stuff" purchased for the family. There is, to most men, a solemnity in this act, which deters them from performing it as long as possible, but it lifted a great weight from the heart of Mr. Haxton, and thenceforth he seemed to be happier than he was ever known to be before.

When he met Mary Winthrop, he always patted her head, and called her "pretty Molly," which made her heart bound with the remembrance of his first token of the safety of the wanderer; and somehow she felt that there was a strong compact between them, unspoken and uncomprehended by those about them, but very precious to both.

The school was still kept by Winthrop, and Mary felt glad when she was required to take the school-room for a day or week, for then there was a change in the bitter current of her thoughts.

The house was falling somewhat into a worn-out aspect, though it had seen but few years. It had been too elaborately carved by inexperienced hands, and the sash of the little windows would scarcely have held together against the winds, if it were not a school-room. They seem so tolerant of abuses—school-houses do—and stand upright under all sorts of unfortunate trials. Perpetuity seems to be an attribute of these rough temples, the elements of mutability being left to the sole use and appropriation of the genius who ministers therein, which are sometimes his or her only virtue. There was a serrate moulding about the edges of the desks which might or might not be considered beautiful, according to the taste of the beholder, but certainly the same finish was not so comfortable on the borders of the benches, provided the occupants possessed short fat pedal extremities which could not touch the floor, and lift their soft surfaces from the carving. Many a chubby child would have asserted that they might be ornamental, but were far from being agreeable.

## CHAPTER XI.

"Sweetly decked with pearly dew
 The morning rose may blow;
But cold successive noontide blasts
 May lay its beauties low.
  \* \* \* \* \*
Dread Omnipotence, alone,
 Can heal the wound he gave;
Can point the brimful grief-worn eyes
 To scenes beyond the grave."

THROUGH the thoughtfulness of John Haxton, the Log House and its perquisites were offered to Mary Winthrop the following summer, which she accepted very thankfully. The days ebbed faster and fairer for her toil. She was amazingly successful, and in her wanderings for her board, as it was not only for the interest of the occupants of the Log House to be an eating itinerant, but it was his or her duty to vary the monotony of the inhabitants in this wise, she accomplished much good. Guy Foster knew how valuable an accessory she was to his mission, and blessed God for her. With that strange heroism which many of the ministers of Christ possess, he would, if need be, lay aside his own tastes and preferences to secure a helpmeet who could labor effectually in this vineyard, but here was one whom he could love with his whole heart, and who was eminently qualified for his holy work. He knew how earnest and sincere she was as a Christian, and he never doubted but she would take the yoke, if it was offered to her, as an especial pleasure and honor. He did not consider his own capabilities to win her affections; he was too enthusiastic in his work for that; and felt that he had been divinely called into the service, and that every one who added to his efficacy would and ought to thank God for the same opportunity.

And when after prayerful consideration of the matter, he approached Mary with his prerequisite attentions, she shrunk from him as a bereaved wife might who had loved devotedly, and the grave was not yet green, or as one who has been secretly and sacredly plighted. His work in life so blinded him that nothing of her manner or words touched his understanding, and he groped his way onward with the pleasurable encouragement of the good father and mother, until, from long seeking of a proper opportunity, he became impatient, and entering the school-room as the afternoon sun lay aslant the rough floor, and the smaller children had kissed their beloved teacher's cheek, he waited until she was alone. She was in that miserable state of sympathetic sorrow which any tender and true-hearted woman feels, when she is conscious an explanation is approaching which will bring unhappiness to one who would bestow upon her the honor of honest affection and life-long devotion. She would have spared him the pain of a refusal, if it were possible, but there was no escape now, and she knew the arguments she would have to meet, and she nerved herself for the contest which she was certain would end in dissatisfaction to both.

"Mary, perhaps you know why I am here this evening. I have tried in vain, Providence seeming to postpone the matter, to speak with you alone. You see how the Lord is crowning my work and sealing my mission to this people, and as in His wisdom he has decreed that it was not good for man to be alone, I have turned my eyes in every direction for a suitable person to share the glory of my calling with me, and your face has come between me and all others, and I take it as a Divine direction. Will you be my wife?"

Her voice trembled. She did not like this way of putting the question. It stung her conscience, but did not touch her heart, and her pity ebbed away with the flush that had at first mounted to her cheek.

"First, Mr. Foster, tell me why you think me fittest to take this position."

"Because, my friend, your own work is so blest, and you are more to my little church than any one now. Encouraging the timid, leading the stray ones, and teaching the ignorant, is your mission."

"If I can do this and am performing such good works as you attribute to me, then am I in the right way now, and no change of outer circumstances will better my ways and purposes."

He saw his error and then permitted his heart to speak. "I am very lonely, Mary, and you have become very dear to me since I have been among this people—come with me and make me happy in the sunshine of your sweet face, always—I love you, Mary," and he held his hands imploringly to her.

This touched her woman's nature, and she said, regretfully:—

"I can not, Mr. Foster, I have no affection to return for yours. Not that you are unworthy, but my heart is preoccupied—it is wholly another's, nor have I any expectation of being happier for its bestowal; but it is irrevocable. I wish you had not so honored me."

"Mary, is it possible you can love a man whom you can not respect? Does your heart follow one who escaped the penalty of the law of man, but can not fly from that of God?" he asked with a touch of severity in his tones.

"He has gone from the penalty of a crime he never committed, and God has been with and blessed him; and I do not blush to say that though he never asked for my love, yet in his sorrow and shame it is his entirely and shall be for ever. I respect your zeal for your church and sympathize with it; and I pitied you, a sentiment next to love, before you forgot yourself so much as to disregard the possibilities of innocence in one in whom you *knew* there was no guile, by the measure of your own capabilities of wrong. But for this, I would have thanked you in my heart for the crown of love you would have laid upon my unworthy head."

This was said with a startling vehemence which he did not imagine she possessed, and she hastened from the room. It was with her, in the defence of her absent friend, as it is sometimes with gentler animals, all docility till their loved and cherished are disturbed, and then implacable ferocity takes possession of them. There was enough determination in her manner to have played the daughter of the Siberian Exile. So tragic, so unlike her old self was this phase of her character, that he almost felt relieved that she had rejected him. He feared her—those sparkling eyes had so dilated and flashed! Providence had watched over and cared for him, so he thought, and he thanked heaven then and there for what would have seemed a fearful disappointment had the result even been a matter of doubt one hour before. It was all ended and endured, yet with his belief in depravity he found he had fancied women were angelic, made of a tithe of finer material than common sinning men, and this dispersion of the ideal halo with which he had surrounded them, made him feel sadly miserable. In his absorbing love for his great mission, he could not comprehend how it was that every sincere Christian should not feel the same holy zeal, and lay down all other human emotions a required sacrifice to this one glorious work of the ministry. He walked home with his destiny looking him stoutly and steadily in the face, and yet with meekness he returned it, yet it may be a few manly tears fell as he watched the pleasant vision fade and heard his sentence.

Alone!

Thenceforward there should be nothing to divide his love, nothing to halve his sorrows or share his burdens and his joys. Mary might have been severe, and so are all who suffer. Few are sweet when the cup of which they drink is continually bitter. Think of this, ye who judge harshly of those who utter stinging words. Perhaps sorrow has left them no pleasant thoughts.

Certainly she had never been so miserable as now. The grief which lay sluggish and chill in her own heart had never touched another before. She was too pitiful, too loving to lay her burden upon any one, or divide it by seeking sympathy. Her mother understood her too well to seek to know more than her womanly nature would bestow unasked; but when the young pastor came no more in the summer evenings, and his face looked old and worn, and his lips thinner and compressed, his voice sunk to a minor key from its wonted full tones, she needed no words, and was very sorrowful. Her husband was tenderer to his daughter, and stroked her long hair till the tears came, and were brushed away in silence from both faces; but not a thought was syllabled by either, of the great sorrow that threatened to shadow Mary's young life, and brush its wing over their own, through their love for her.

In her school she was more earnest, and more devoted to her Sunday scholars; more zealous and saint-like; and John Haxton looked wistfully at the girl and changed his appellation of "pretty Molly," to "poor Mary," and his patting to a close clasp of her pale little hand.

\* \* \* \* \* \*

One Sunday, about a year after the departure of Benjamin Rollin, Mary saw a strange glimmer in the eyes of the man, as he gazed at her with a sort of nervous pleasure which made her entirely oblivious of the sermon of the pastor, whose text was from those inspired proverbs of the wise man: "A good name is rather to be chosen than great riches;" and again, "The memory of the just is blessed, but the name of the wicked shall rot."

Mary heard this, and after the first flush of indignation had died down, she felt sure that the young clergyman meant to be kind to her, and that he felt that there was a sore place in her heart, that to cauterize with a fierce hand would bring pain, but afterward would cause sweet healing. She had seen the expressive eyes of

John Haxton, and knew he had some word for her of comfort and consolation, and so the caustic of the sermon was like a wordless lullaby, in which her soul swayed backward to the past and forward to a far but beautiful future.

She lingered a little that her friend might catch her ear, and all he said was, "Molly, it's prosperous times on the Mississippi, and I was to say so to you. Chirk up, pretty Molly," and passed on to his home. Oh, how beautiful that dawning autumn looked to that young girl! It wove its arabesques of beauty over the hills and meadows, winding its web of gorgeous coloring along the vine-draped fences, touching the bordering of the brooks, and mingling with it all, was a prophecy to her heart that a second summer would come to her life, more lovely and satisfying even than the first. Spring is charming, but it is only a promise; but autumn is grandly glorious, for it is a fulfillment of the year's mission.

After this a new order of things was inaugurated in the Log School House. The lads of its first winter were young men now, and they had "ciphered through the 'Western Calculator,' and got answers to all the sums;" and therefore, in their own estimation, were eminently calculated to assume the profession of teacher, and bear the scepter of the Ridge School. They would do it cheap—the honor was something—and so Nelson Winthrop retired. He had borne the pioneer's burden, and now that the way was smoother and easier, others took the path and crowded him aside. He was not cynical; he did not murmur and ask his soul in bitterness, "Where is the good of it?" but could with a modern poet,

"Turn the past's mirror backward—its shadows removed,
  The dim, confused mass becomes softened, sublime:
I have worked, I have felt, I have lived, I have loved,
  And each was a step towards the goal I now climb,
Thou, God, thou sawest the good of it!"

His reputation as a scholar and a good man, reached the inhabitants of the nearest village, and he was called to them, to instruct their children. He felt that it would be a broader life for him and his children; and so he sold his little farm, and entered his new home with a wonderful enthusiasm. Mary did not like to go from old associations and sweet and bitter memories; but it was wrong and foolish to brush the sparkle of pleasure from the cup of her father's happiness, and so with a promise from John Haxton to see her when there was any *reason* for it, and to secure for her the summer schools, she parted from her old friends, amid the tears of Sandy McLain, and the appearance of a severe cold in the head of Mr. Haxton. His banner-like bandana handkerchief was in constant requisition as he blustered about, attending to the moving matters, with a don't-care sort of swagger in his manner, but a do-care in his rapidly winking eyes. He thought he had deceived everybody, and that nobody would know, so he said to himself, "What an old-womanish sort of fool I am!" He told his wife he would " e'enamost as soon have been bearer to a funeral."

Sandy was quite crushed, till a bright idea struck him. He would go to town himself and learn a trade, and then he could enjoy his dear books and evenings. And as he had Greek, Hebrew, and Latin at night, and leather by day, his proficiency in the last business never lifted him to eminence in the trade.

## CHAPTER XII.

> "Like lamps in Eastern sepulchres,
> Amid my heart's deep gloom,
> Affection sheds its holiest light
> Upon my husband's tomb.
> And as those lamps, if brought once more
> To upper air, grow dim,
> So my soul's love is cold and dead,
> Unless it glow for him."

THIS winter passed swiftly in the novelty of the new life, and the teacher's pretty daughter was surrounded with admirers who were fascinated by her loveliness, and frozen by her indifference to their attentions. She was beloved by her girlish companions, and in turn she found intense pleasure in the society of her sex, a delight she had never experienced before, save in that of her mother. But the spring found her mistress of the Old Log School House, and a steady member of Mrs. Walton's family. This was a remarkable concession on the part of the district, but the new appreciation which the Winthrop family had found, lifted them in the estimation of their country people not a little. Mary found in Mrs. Walton a new friend, one who often mentioned that name which was spoken no more in their own household, and who religiously believed that the time would come when the banished one would return, full of honor and happiness to gladden his old friends. These were like the words of a seer to the girl, and she let herself be very happy in the hope of another added to her own. Guy Foster met her now with that unworldly face and manner of his, as if only soul spoke to soul, and there were no other relations in life. She pitied him, and but for the fear of bringing his dead hope to life, she would have offered him her friendship and assistance, whenever a woman's words and a woman's soft footfalls are needed in the sorrowing ways of mortal life. But she had learned a little of the subtle changes of the heart of man, and stood aloof from him.

One evening after her school-room door was closed for the night, and she was slowly wending her way across the bridge toward the mill, Charlie Haxton came out from the sound of the wheel, and for the first time in his life walked beside her toward Mrs. Walton's little home. His face wore the insignia of drunken debauchery, and she shuddered; but with the resoluteness of her character, controlled her expressions of disgust, and received his salutations with quiet friendliness. She knew he did not visit the mill now, and could not but conclude it was for this especial interview that he came. There had been remorseful thoughts and their questionings haunting him of late, and that instinctive fear which attends guilt like a servant. He thought perhaps some strange coincidence which sometimes reveals things hidden, might yet betray him, and if he sounded the depths of Mary's knowledge of the affair cautiously, he might re-assure himself, or exorcise the demon of speculation.

"It seems like old times to see you, Mary—those old days in the Log School House, eh? Don't you mind 'em? There's your father and that Scotch boy off to town; 'Silly' in her grave, poor thing! Robert Winthrop grown to be such a manly fellow, and living away in the far West,—and only a few left besides you and me. Do you ever get sorry about old times, Mary?"

"No, Charlie, old times are pleasant to remember—except that all have not made good men and women who were scholars there," she said, looking hard into his face.

He thought she meant Benjamin, and not for one instant did his soul's accuser stir in his sluggishness to say, "Thou art the man," and so he jumped at the conclusion too quickly.

"Yes, there was Benny. 'Twas a pity of him; he was so keen with his books."

"What was a pity?" she asked, turning upon him abruptly, and disconcerting him not a little.

"Why,—you know the trouble about Peter Dally's mother, to be sure."

"Charlie Haxton, he did not commit that crime. I know who did, and so does one other, and it will all be revealed before very long. Wait with patience, and the punishment will be awarded."

She stood before him like an accusing angel, with her golden brown hair lighting her brow, as if it had been a halo, her face whitened with emotion, and her eyes like fire.

"Oh, Mary—don't," was all he said, and she waited a little, and he turned back to the mill, and she walked on. She did not feel any surer of the innocence of her friend—she could not—but she felt more hopeful for the future and its possible revelations from the troubled answer, "Mary, don't." He did not think of the one she mentioned, but fancied she spoke of some other who might have witnessed the deed, and was, like himself, mortal, and subject to the rules of expediency. Instead of obtaining comfort from the interview, he was utterly miserable, and lived in anxious fear of exposition. To drown the tormenting fiend, he took deeper draughts of the fiery cup, and scarcely permitted a moment of natural thought.

Sometimes days passed during which his mother never saw his face. She wept some, grew more and more irritable, and with renewed vigor, endeavored to forget her sorrows in the pleasure of scrubbing and dusting.

The next two years passed with a miserable master in the School House, who, if such sweet influence could be forgotten, or such thorough teaching obliterated, would have swept out the summer's impressions from the souls of the children, and left only the remembrance of struggles for supremacy, boisterous frolic, and vague instruction in matters which were foggy to the professor of Belles-Lettres, who had mastered the "Western Calculator," and could write a little, and read less and nothing more.

One winter morning, John Haxton was found dead, having been killed by the hoof of a vicious horse. It was a thrilling event. The strong current of sorrow which ran through every heart in his neighborhood, attested how much he had grown in their affections during the last few years of his life. To all it was a bereavement, but to Mary Winthrop it was the severing of the connecting link between herself and the dearly beloved absent. It was very like a dual death to her, and she sorrowed almost without hope. Providence held a dark vail over her future. Nelson Winthrop and his family attended the funeral, which act of Christian sympathy was more soothing to the bereaved ones than any thing that happened, but afterward became a sore spot in memory.

There had been a will left, and to the amazement of every one, one half of his large property was bestowed unconditionally upon Mary Winthrop, and with it, the care of Peter Dally,—a sealed letter to be delivered unopened to the aforesaid girl. She was awed by the strange intelligence, and felt it to be a burden laid upon her, and afflicting to those who had the right to expect whatever he left behind him,—but the letter explained it all. To her father, even, she did not feel at liberty to confide its contents, and he was curious, as a matter of course, but content in the belief that she would do right. Charles was almost frantic with anger. His share of the fortune was put into the hands of trustees to be dealt to him during his lifetime, and then to go wholly to his sister, as if it were impossible for him to survive Silly, which was true.

All the money, the mill, and the farm detached from his homestead, and which surrounded the School House, belonged to the young teacher. Her father believed that a man had no moral right to bestow his fortune in such an apparently whimsical manner, and wished Mary to refuse its acceptance, but she only said,

"Father, I have no right to cast it away from me. Sometime you will comprehend the mystery." It was a still stranger thing than the bequeathing of the wealth, the way in which it was used. Mary rented the grounds to practical farmers, the mill to Mr. Walton, as a sheltered employment suited his delicate health; and Peter was to reside with the latter, as she could not take him to a village life with his idiosyncracies.

The death of Mr. Haxton had almost consoled the poor, strange fellow who had partially forgotten his earlier sorrows, and Mary had him provided for bountifully, with the liberty of labor or idleness; but she touched not a coin of her new income herself. She continued her school, spent her small earnings economically, and toiled on. Her old friends said she had learned to love gold with the possession, and was miserly and selfish; but they did not know. She had latterly lived with her Uncle Abel Winthrop, when she was teaching, as the old enemy had lured him into forgetfulness of the crippled hand and the fearful storm, and she could comfort the poor family.

This summer, as if the avenger of wrong was busy with his errands of sorrow, her Uncle Abel Winthrop was called to his last account.

He had gone with his wife to visit their oldest daughter in the country far down the Ohio, and the hearts of husband and wife were elate with joy at the anticipated pleasure of a family meeting. They had reached a city on the river shore, where the steamer tarried for a single hour. Here Abel wandered out to the street, and in the forgetfulness of self, in the midst of temptation, he touched, tasted, and became intoxicated! With brain ruled by the spirit of which he too sadly partook, he attempted to return to his wife, who impatiently and tearfully awaited his coming on board the steamer, but he fell from the plank into the swift current, and went to judgment!

And his loving wife saw his face no more.

The grave of a Christian was denied him by this fearful providence, and she, poor wife! mourned him, as if he had been all to her that her girlish dreams had pictured. Poor Abel Winthrop!

Close upon the steps of this shadow came another. Mr. Winthrop's death had startled the dram-drinkers, and they were making new resolutions of reform. The stoutest of these was Charles Haxton; with that will which he inherited from his father, when he determined upon a purpose he never turned back. He would drink no more, he said to himself, but his resolve came too late! That sentence, *too late!* had been the knell whose sad refrain has beat upon many a despairing soul. "When he would have repented he could not," might have been engraven upon his tomb-stone. That terrible visitor to heated brains, Delirium Tremens, bore him, after a few days of pitiful suffering, to his long home. It is to be hoped that, "after life's fitful fever he sleeps well."

Peter was the only one whose nerves could long endure the frightful spectacle, and he, with the heroism of love, not for the man who writhed before him, but for the memory he cherished, waited all the long nights and slowly creeping days of his anguish, patient till the rest came, with an almost superhuman endurance.

The strange things the wild man uttered might mean much, or they might be the conjurings of the demon who tormented him. His mother—sad creature! thought nothing; but there were questioning looks flung from one gaze to another by those who surrounded him,— kindly neighbors who were brothers indeed in times of trouble in those thinly inhabited places. "Tread lightly on the ashes of the dead," was their sentiment, and so their thoughts remained unspoken. Now that Charles Haxton had died without revealing the secret he had so long concealed, there was little hope left for Mary that the dear name she loved so well would ever shine out purified from the stain cast upon it; but when the cloud seemed darkest, light dawned, and the truth was vindicated.

It was after one of her depressed and hopeless days, that it happened. She was too sad, even with her sweet forgetfulness of self, to spend that night with the continued crooning of sobs from the breaking heart of her aunt, haunting her sleep, and she went to her friend, Mrs. Walton. It was a charming evening, such as draw dreamers from the shelter of roofs, and make them bare their heads to the stars; and the restless feet of the girl took her out into the pretty garden which was Peter's especial pet. Mary had never inquired of any one about the death of Charlie, for she thought if that which she most wished spoken had found utterance, justice would have parted the lips of the hearers. She had been written down an enemy to the house of Haxton, when the will was read, and had not received recognition afterward; so her sympathies were not offered to the stricken family, as it would have pained them to look into her innocent face.

"Peter, sit down and tell me about poor Charlie, and what troubled his last hours so fearfully."

"O Mary, I've kept it so long, it don't signify now. I wouldn't let on while his father was out of the grave, and there's no use on it now; but 'twas dreadful hard for poor Peter. Sometimes I thought the old man knowed it all, he was so good and feelin' like to me, a poor silly lad—no, I wouldn't let on."

"Peter, my father and I were your first friends; can you not trust me? It is better that you should tell some one who knows what is most suitable for you to do with your secret, and you may injure some one else by keeping what you know locked away in your own heart. Tell me, Peter, do."

There was something so touching, so beseeching in her tone, that a more reasonable soul than Peter's would have yielded to its imploring.

"I saw him do it, Mary," burst from his lips, as if in the unburdening of his guarded secret, there was a lessening of the painful tension about his grieved heart, "I saw it, and it made the fever come which poor Benjie nursed me with, and then never came back any more. Good Benjie!"

How her heart leaped up and exulted in the light that flooded her soul! But she steadied her voice to say:—

"Peter, people said Benjamin Rollin disturbed your poor mother, and the good young man was obliged to go far away among strangers to save himself from punishment, and we have all sorrowed over him more than any words can ever tell."

"Did they say that, Mary? God knows and I know that Charles Haxton took the dead mother of poor Peter from the grave and hid her I can not tell where, for the blindness and the pain came before I could speak to him.

I heard him say to the man who helped him, 'It is a dreadful job, but I can't drive the dog away.' Benjamin Rollin was reading in the kitchen when I went up into the loft, but he did not see me; if he had spoken, I should have told him all. It was so hard to keep it, but Mr. Haxton was so good to me, and he looked so sorry for all Charlie did, sometimes, that I could not make him any more trouble."

"Peter, would you tell this, to let Benjie come home again?"

"Oh, Mary, you are right, and I'll do any thing you say;" and so it happened that the truth was at last revealed, and the kindness shown long before to the poor idiotic lad, was now to be recompensed. "As ye sow, so shall ye reap." If Mary had been tearless in her sorrow, she was softened now, and a night of glad weeping followed those years of sad waiting.

Mrs. Walton wrote to the far off home of Dr. Rollin, as the letter of John Haxton had directed, and oh! how slowly the days came and closed away with their blank faces, until the message that heralded his coming was laid in Mary's expectant palm! Her spirit was tranced into that strange hush which comes over an imaginative and loving spirit, when such a missive, looked for and and longed for, is in our clasp! It was destiny to her. All her future lay in its lines, and it was with no little heroism that she roused herself to meet even its words: "Mary, I am coming. A few, whose lives are vibrating between the half open portals of the grave, and the beseeching call of affection, will keep me for a little while; but when God wills, I shall be with you. Mary, *my* Mary!"

Then she knew how good, and true, and tender he was, and felt repaid ten thousand fold for all her sorrow. When the autumn came, that time of especial good to her, Benjamin Rollin stood before her, and she asked nothing more of joy than the gladness his presence brought her, with his name purified, and his old friends more regardful because of all they had thought of wrong in him. Peter's story and the revelations of the death-bed were enough, but the lesson had its uses in making them less eager to believe evil of any one.

Yes, the autumn had come, and very like the one which saw the Old Log School House rise from the barren ground in one day's sunshine, was this one. The earth looked as if fairy-fingers had woven Gobelin tapestry all over its surface, and netted it with scarlet and amber meshes, like a gaudy vail.

Guy Foster softened, and with tears, real human tears, craved pardon for his doubt of the young Doctor's veracity and honor, and when Rollin took the hand of his old master, he heard these trembling, touching words:

"May the Good Father judge us hereafter; we are blind and erring, and know not what we do. My son, let the past be forgiven, forgotten."

When Guy Foster had said the solemn words which united these beautiful lives, though his lips quivered, he told Dr. Rollin how he had tried to win Mary to himself, but she had been faithful and loving always in her silence, and though he had felt that she was not a Christian to reject him with such bitterness, yet he comprehended it all now. He was blinded by his wishes, and saw not as God sees, and he thanked Him for keeping the good girl's heart steadfast in her truth.

This was noble in the young pastor, but it was his one selfish dream of a lifetime, and though he would have been softer in his manners, tenderer in his rebukes, and sweeter in his sympathies, if a wife had made his life more human, and little children had nestled in his arms and heart; yet he fulfilled all the duties which came to him as a faithful servant, and died at last, early called to rest, with the assurance that his ministry had been accepted of God. Through his brief period of labor, Dr. and Mrs. Rollin were his warmest friends. Mr. Foster was an admirer of Christian song, and always seemed happy in mingling his voice with those of his singing brethren and sisters in the Lord. One of his favorite songs was:—

> "I'm a pilgrim, and I'm a stranger,
> I can tarry, I can tarry but a night;
> Do not detain me, for I am going,
> To where the streamlets are ever flowing,
> I'm a pilgrim, and I'm a stranger,
> I can tarry, I can tarry but a night."

And on his dying bed he was cheered by the sweet song-promise that fell like honeyed dew-drops on his soul, just before the bright day-dawn of immortality:—

> "And I soon will be over on the other side of Jordan,
> Hallelujah!"

## CHAPTER XIII.

"Some are in the church-yard laid,
   Some sleep beneath the sea;
But few are left of our old class,
   Excepting you and me;
And when our time is come, dear friend,
   And we are called to go,
I hope they'll lay us where we played,
   Some twenty years ago."

BENJAMIN ROLLIN had faced a peculiar destiny, and one, too, that the Good Father above had sent to him— a good, distilled through evil—a sweet draught from a lipped leaf-cup of rue. It had enlarged his thoughts, and taught him, in his isolation, to ponder those questions so vital to the heart and life of society; and from his study, uninterrupted by the seducing ripples from the placid streams of social life, he had evolved philosophic conclusions which he applied to the lives of those over whom he had acquired such absolute control. The energies bestowed upon a needy people would have been expanded almost entirely within the circle around which his loving heart, with centripetal force, revolved. The centrifugal, by habit and culture, was now able to balance his interests, as became a worker in God's world, and he did not sink to a mere seeker after individual happiness. He saw the subtle working of indolence among the people. He saw, boy as he was, the great truth that the hands must be busy, if they would commit no sin; that idle thoughts generate evil purposes; that to clothe the body and feed the craving appetite of man, were not enough to make them great or good, though he brought them even to this, from their lethargy, when he came among them, led by the unseen Hand which he clasped blindly in that first great darkness. Questionings from his young brain had lain like leaden weights upon his heart in those first years, but the answers wise and practical, and freighted with good to that debased community, dawned like an apocalypse upon his asking thoughts, and like an ambitious and careful builder he reared the superstructure upon which other workers piled the edifice of a society, than which a better is not known even now on all the borders of that mighty stream of waters. He thanked God for the fate that seemed at first so fearful. When he was ready for a little rest, peace, and happiness, they came to him affluently. Not the rest of idleness, but the rest of the heart and the satisfaction in required toil. The two, now united, had suffered and waited, omitting nothing of duty that came to them, and had lived to see this fair dawning of a beautiful life. Who should follow them, and take up the dropped threads of their unfinished work, God knows, and labor is never done. Theirs had been like the path through the snow.

> " Narrow and rough it lies between
> Wastes where the wind creeps, biting keen;
> Every step of the slippery road
> Marks where a weary foot has trod—

Who'll go!—who'll go?
After the rest on the path through the snow?"

Mary, beautiful Mary, with the lines which sorrow had written on her face, obliterated,—rounded out by happiness, gave up the helm she had held, only too gladly, with the dead man's letter, leaving her husband now to perform, as he chose, the office of steward. The letter with all its faults and quaintness made tears brim the eyes of the reader, and here it is. Perhaps it may be supposed that such a man ought to have given ground for the Old Log School House.

"MY DEAR MOLLY:—

i shal be ded when you rede this leter. i rite it to sa that i wish you and Benny to hav haf my property—i no how it is tho you don't say nothin betwixt you. He didn't do that thing no more nor you and i did and it will all come out sumtime.—God wont let it stay as it is—i hav my own notion about it, and you and him ort to hav kompensashun from my family. He was a good boy and I liked him more nor all the wurld at last. He is in Acton Missippi. rite to him when the truth comes out, take good keer of Peter—Be true to Benny, from yure
luvin and ded friend
JOHN HAXTON."

So because it was not wholly hers, Mary could not reject the lands bestowed upon her, though in her heart at the time, she longed to cast them back into the hands of the rightful heirs.

Mrs. Haxton had welcomed Benny, as she still called him, as if he were all that was left of her broken household to come back to her. She knew now how he had suffered from her son, and when he offered to return to her the estate that he felt would burden him, because of the good already uncancelled of years agone, she begged him to let her feel that it paid him in some degree for his long banishment, and so it was decided; and he took his sweet bride to his far-away home, where the people who loved him, longed to see his face again. He had been prospered, and there had been great changes in the little low town. Another dispensation had been inaugurated under his guidance, and the fevers came no more. Tidiness, rational ways of living, and sanitary measures had lifted them in the scale of being.

It is a singular fact, and one not easily reconciled to our established notions of inherent depravity, that filthiness and want produce sin, and the lowest range of crimes. Cleanliness with poverty seldom does. An irreverent but facetious writer has said that, "Soap had done as much for civilization as Christianity." One fact is undeniable, that cleanliness and Christianity go hand in hand, and both must reach the heart and come from the heart. Let a man be clean clear through, and he will be apt to be a good man.

Mary had parted from her home with tears and smiles so closely intermingled, that it was difficult to tell which predominated; but she soon became the happy angel of mercy to the strange people about her, and the star of the "sweet home" of Dr. Rollin.

And here endeth as much as the writer may tell of the one tragic romance of the Old Log School House. There were other romances of which the public knew nothing; but they were the most wonderful in the world to the two immediately concerned. Every heart has its own, and we often fall to speculating what it may be or has been, so cold and common-place do the actors seem.

Aramintha Haxton never married. Peter has become

an inseparable portion of Mrs. Walton's family, and is happy and useful, and we hope hereafter there will be apportioned him a blessed immortality.

Nelson Winthrop is still in his armor, and laboring for his generation, and for those who are to follow. He has sent out into the world many a noble man, with the highest aspirations of Christian manhood glowing within him; and his son, who began his career in the Old Log School House, is a pilgrim-teacher to-day, happy in the calling and in the company of those to whom his mission is more especially directed, the children of the land. His only ambition is to be useful in an humble way in teaching truth and love to the rising generation, to many thousands of whom his lessons, gathered from the experience of many friends, and happily arranged, are sent statedly to the North, the South, the East, and the West.

The old door-sill is thin and uneven; the upper lip of the mammoth fire-place is drooped with age and its burden, and perhaps a little sullenness because there is a modern stove standing before it, grim and unsocial, and taunting the fire-dogs with its assumption of improvement. But it is a practical age, and the roar of the hidden fire within its closed doors, is but in keeping with the clamor of science smouldering and moaning for speech, and only here and there bursting out to dazzle us.

Sandy McLain has lifted his huge head into a professor's chair, and expounds Hebrew to the edification of the students of a popular College. He gained it, mostly, by the cabinet bench of the lame teacher, who persisted in pleasing himself with his mechanic's tools till old age stiffened his nimble and cunning fingers. Sandy was a goodly boy, and people say Prof. McLain is a goodly man.

Mrs. Abel Winthrop found peace with the touches of time, but it lingered long before its coming. Her dear eldest son has taken her home with him to the far West, and their little farm, just over the hill, south-westerly from the Old Log School House, has been sold to a neighboring farmer, whose acres are increasing with his years. The popular leaning toward good—that good whose leaven was gathered in the Old Log School House —has lightened and *enlightened* the whole lump. Near where the distillery once poured forth its poison for both soul and body, a pretty stone church stands and points its spire, like a steady white finger, to the upper and changeless habitation. The dews lie over many who have fallen by the tempter. One still walks the earth stricken with age, and as remorse has its "indisputable lettering" on human faces, so can all read the retribution of this once influential but now forsaken man. He has some kind traits almost covered up in his eccentricities, and not unfrequently a sigh for the eventful past and its mournful associations will escape from his bosom. His head is frosted already in the cold and chilly autumn of his career, and soon will snowy winter shroud him in the death-slumber. May God constrain him to think about his soul's welfare, and forgive him and those who may have judged him even too severely, all their sins!

Where the rude cabins once sent up their smoke from broad hearthstones, now are seen handsome and comfortable dwellings, and the touch of prosperity is visible everywhere. But the Old Log School House which is still perched on its corner of soil, as yellow and barren as in early times, rears its stone-chimney, though not so proudly, for the storms have lessened its hight by many a stone, and the windows rattle in the winter wind, like bones from which the plumpness of youthful flesh has fallen, and the shingles are curled and imbricated, and the tears of summer rain and the jewels of the winter snow, fall on the heads of the young children.

How or why this one relic stands in the midst of plenty, and by the side of garnished homes, it might be unkind to say. Let us think it is the memories it brings, a sacred respect for the past and its retrospections, and not the disregard of the people for that good which exalted them to their present elegant prosperity. Surely the souls of their children would not be permitted to take shape from such surroundings, because of acquisitiveness—the love of getting and keeping gold, oh, no!

The mind of the young is moulded from what it sees, as well as what it hears; and if symmetry of thought and loveliness of character be the one most coveted thing for the soul-blossoms that unfold in our home sanctuaries, then should the rough walls be made smooth and fair, and softness and delicacy take the place of unsightly angularity, comfort be taken in exchange for rude disagreeables, and now and then a beautiful picture should be suspended to take the child's thought to the charming spots of God's earth, or to the grand deeds of some of. His children.

True, a poor house is better than no place in which to gather the little ones and teach them the upward way, but the marked contrast between the houses and the shapes of the spring whence the young souls draw their draughts of the cup of wisdom, is too suggestive of temporal instead of spiritual culture. It makes the little thinkers believe that, after all, the growth of the soul is of little import compared with the growth of purse and power.

Children, the wisdom hoarded in these precious young years of yours is the talisman of happiness, greatness, power, aye, and even of gold; but there is a something beyond this which is vailed to us now, but the vesture that wraps the immortal will be rent, perhaps too soon for us all. The dews may be gathering this very hour, which will lie upon our still faces, and the air growing still with the ceasing of our voices—who can tell?

Gather the good while it is falling, be the surroundings what they may. Prepare to work, to be rulers if you can in the strife of existence; and subalterns if you must, but be faithful always, then shall sweet peace like drops of cool water to a fevered lip, or tender memories like a swarm of singing birds caroling in a pleasant dream, be yours, and the smile of the Good Father light your darkest hours.

Many there be who remember the Old Log School House with a quick thrill rushing through the soul, and the sound of the words we call it by, is like having one's Christian name spoken long after it is lost in household silence, and the curl of its letters strange to the pen. The formal title, or the brief signature, have obliterated it, but an old friend utters it like an echo from long past years—sweet, sunny years!

"My Christian name, my Christian name,
I never hear it now:

> None have the right to utter it,
> 'Tis lost, I scarce know how:
> My worldly name the world speaks loud,
> Thank God for well-earned fame!
> But silence sits at my cold, cold hearth—
> I have no household name."

So sang one who felt the loss of its soft utterance. But the Old Log School House we can call up ourselves, and it has a holy claim upon memory. In a few fleeting years this hallowed old temple will have crumbled away for ever, and the generations to come shall only know that such edifices as this were ever called school houses. We would here pay a tribute of kindest regard to Old Log School Houses all. And when these soul-houses of ours are taken down by the hand of the Destroyer, may we be blessed in the remembrance that we learned to love our mates as our own lives, and God supremely, even under the roof of the Old Log School House. Then may our latest thought be a loving thought, and when the body's pulse is still, may the spirit be ready-winged for the upward flight into the regions of the blest, where there is a "house not made with hands, eternal in the heavens," where all our dear departed school-mates are companioned with angels, and where the Great Teacher will welcome his scholars home!

Teachers who have felt almost ready to lay down the armor of their warfare against ignorance, when discomfort brooded about them, and vile influences drove them with fierce tauntings to look to some easier path with pleasanter duties, and yet turned a deaf ear to the allurings, and steadfast, level eyes to the toil, when the evening shadows came and the dull surgings of the dividing river were heard not far off, remember the Old Log School House as the spot where the heavenly crown was won—that crown in waiting to encircle the brow. Toil, teacher! Sow the good seed!

> "Plant it—all thou canst, with prayers,
> Should He need a goodly tree
>   For the shelter of the nations,
> He will make it grow; if not,
>   Never yet his love forgot,
> Human love and faith and patience."

Always blessed!

One who has filled the highest post of honor in a nation's gift, said, while the white of age was sifted over his head: "Looking backward over the years, I remember nothing with so much satisfaction as those seasons of teaching in obscurity. And when I was in the capitol at Washington, nothing was so pleasant as to have men, who had risen to useful eminence, take my hand and say, 'I was your pupil once!' This was better than popular praise or popular power."

This distinguished man attended school in a log school house in his early life.

> "Who knows what bright October suns
>   May light up distant valleys mild,
> Where, as our pathway downward runs,
>   We see joy meet us as a little child,
> Who, sudden by the roadside stands
>   To kiss the travelers' weary brows,
> And lead them through the twilight lands,
>   Safely unto our Father's house."

Sweet is thy memory, and blessed thy teachings to the giver and receiver, Old Log School House! Thou hast sheltered the head and nourished the soul of many a wanderer up and down the earth; and though unsightly to strange eyes in thy fading glory, yet in our need thou wast all sufficient, and we love thee!

WE LOVE THEE!

# LIFE MUSINGS.

*" We spend our years as a tale that is told."*—Ps. xc. 9.

One pleasant eve in summer time,
As 'neath a weeping willow tree I chanced
To wander, seeking rest and flowers, near
The grave of one beloved, but gone up home
To God—with mother's Bible in my hand
To teach me; while a gentle summer's breeze
Breathed music through the leafy boughs above,
That o'er that grassy mound cast vesper shades,
Solemn with sacred quietude; while spoke
In lute-like tenderness, of calm, serene,
And holy rest, those airy whispers there;
While velvet roses shed their sweet perfume
On every zephyr-breath; while gladsome songs
Of forest-warblers echoed through the deep
Recesses of the neighb'ring grove; while far
In some still solitude, the plaintive coo
Of the lone turtle-dove faintly was heard,
Mingling with nearer notes elate with love—
The notes of robins; while the toiling bee,
With a lulling, low, monotonous tune
Was gleaning honey from the clover-tops
That bloomed and blushed in beauty all around;
*While nature chorused all her harmonies—*
'Twas then life seemed an earnest of itself,
More glorious in heaven!

                    I am
*Not* glad that I am born to die! and sink
Into the chilling coldness of the grave;
To lie embraced by Death's strong, sullen grasp,
In that dark vale of rottenness and worms:
But rather would I ever have the bliss
Of living to discern and taste the charms
Of earth,—though transient they may be, and oft
Too sadly mixed with woe.

———————'Twas thus I thought,
When, as to rouse me from such reveries,
A gently waking gale swept by, and woke
The slumbers of my soul, with the low sound
Of pages turning quickly.  God's own hand
Was there, and kindly turned the cov'nant leaves
Of his blest oracle of Truth and Love:
Of mercy rich, and with abundant grace
To wash the stains of sin's most crimson dye—
The only light that shines along the path
That leads the anxious wand'rer through the dark,
Wide wilderness of mortality.  Yet
Methought, as quickly in succession turned
Those precious tablets of God's Holy Law
Before my earnest gaze, that I could read
Dim outline of such words as these:

———————"Lay hold
*On life eternal*—ON ETERNAL LIFE!" *
"For all flesh is grass that withereth—
A flower that fadeth soon away—away!" †
"Lo, the place of thy permanent abode

\* 1 Tim. vi. 12. † Isaiah xl. 6, 8.

## LIFE MUSINGS.

Is a glorious high throne for ever." *
" Behold ! they who *endure* shall be counte
Happy." †

Ah no ! this world, with all its joys,
Is but a hollow, melancholy dream,
Compared to what shall be " WORLD WITHOUT END."
Ever sorrowing, troubling, dying, here ;
This can not be th' abiding place of souls.

\* \* \* \* \* \*     Oh ! is there not
Some fairer heritage of joy than this,
Where life is not a shadow, wan and dim ?
Where choirs seraphic sing their choral hymns
Unmarred by harsh and mournful wails of grief ?
Where flowers of unfading tints are kissed
By crystal dew-drops from the fount of God ?
Where friends hold fellowship with friends throughout
A vast eternity ! Where we may meet
Our dear ones gone before, and be with them
For ever and for evermore !

'Tis there—
'*Tis there* I long to go.  From weariness,
And toil, and death; to dwell with Him
Who banished from the tomb all fear and dread,
And sweetened that last bitter draught with love,
With undeserved and gracious love.  On Him
I cast myself, undone and lost and lone,
All sinful as I am.  With faith I lean
Upon the promises of *endless* life ;
Of *everlasting* peace—*eternal* rest,
Found written in his Word.

\* Jeremiah xvii. 12.          † James v. 11.

# SUMMERINGS IN CANADA.

July 14th, 1859, was a gala-day at Niagara Falls. Early in the morning the streets were crowded with people from every quarter, all anxious to see the renowned Mons. Blondin perform his airy promenade. It is estimated that twenty-five thousand people were on the banks of the river within sight of the narrow pathway. The afternoon was oppressively warm, and it was actual toil to stand, sit, or lie in the sunshine.

I found a very eligible location on the American side, a few rods up the river from the hither end of the rope. At four o'clock, thousands of eyes were riveted on the high shore from which Blondin was announced to start. At a little before five he started out, backward, towards Canada. His movements were graceful as a bird's, and he seemed but playing on his slender pathway, as a bird plays on a bough!

When he had gone half way across the fearful chasm, he paused, sat down on the rope, and waited until the sprightly little steamer, "Maid of the Mist," came down the river within a few rods of the rope-crossing; he was only waiting to give a distinguished marksman a chance to shoot a pistol ball from the steamer, 200 feet below, through his hat! The boat kept up just steam enough to maintain her position against the swift current, and while the eager spectators were on the tip-toe of excitement and anticipation, the marksman who was standing on the deck of the boat, was observed to raise his arm and point steadily towards Blondin's hat! That moment was one of great suspense. Bang goes the pistol, and down goes—Blondin's hat, attached to a string, and lowered slowly to the "Maid of the Mist," for inspection. Sure enough the ball had passed through it; the mark was there! Blondin then hopped to his rope-way and proceeded. When about three-fourths of the way, he deliberately laid down, with his back to the rope, for a minute or two, then arose and tripped onward again until he reached the Canada shore, safely, amid the cheers and shouts of the multitude. As he neared the British side, the band over there struck up the tune "Get out of the Wilderness;" and played "Hail Columbia," as he stepped upon their soil. He was exactly twenty-four minutes in crossing.

After remaining an hour in Canada, he came a-rope once more, with a wheel-barrow, and trotted that wabbling affair over to Uncle Sam in ten minutes! It was a thrilling sight, and one which I have no curiosity to see repeated. It is criminally foolish to trifle thus with human life. In experiments like this no possible good can result to the community at large. It has no salutary influence, but quite the reverse. Out on the edge of Niagara Falls village, one evening, I observed a young lad perched upon a high board fence, with a long lath in his hands for a balancing pole, and a dozen wondering juveniles round about his heroship. I shouldn't wonder if some "Young Americas" would crack their heedless skulls, in aping the Blondin feat.

Strange that so many are lavish in their congratulations of this *muscular* walking on the narrow way. There is another "straight and narrow path" in which a poor pilgrim may travel with greater honor. It is not a source of worldly enthusiasm to see a pious soul safely journeying over deep and dark dangers, toward the heavenly land. O no! To be a vigilant, faithful, earnest Christian in perilous pilgrimage to the other shore, is not noble in the eyes of the thoughtless world; yet there are angels who rejoice at such faithful adventurers, toiling toward the land of rest.

The "Cave of the Winds," at Niagara Falls, is situated at the foot of the rock, between Goat and Luna Islands, and is one of the most terrific sights on the American side. Near the entrance to the Cave, is a dressing-room, in which we exchanged our ordinary clothing for a cotton bathing suit, coarse shoes, water-proof bonnet, &c., in which uncouth garb we were prepared to get a sound ducking. The gentlemanly guide gave us much valuable information in regard to the Cave, its dimensions, phenomena, and associations, before we entered.

This wonderful cavern has been formed by the constant action of the water upon the soft substratum of the precipice behind the Fall, leaving a dense vault beneath the limestone rock which hangs overhead, thirty feet beyond the base. In front, the transparent falling waters form a mammoth, moving curtain. On account of the tremendous pressure on the atmosphere beneath this arch, the Cave is filled with perpetual, yet ever-varying and raging storms. The war of elements in this watery abyss is fierce and overwhelmingly sublime. Out through the spray, when the sun shines, quivers a beautiful rain-bow.

The Cave is one hundred feet wide, one hundred and thirty feet high, and nearly forty feet deep. Along the rocky and uneven floor of this wild cavern, the spray is hurled violently backward, until it strikes the rough walls of the precipice, then curls upward to the ceiling, thus causing the constant turmoil which gives it the name of the "Cave of the Winds." A hand-railing has been erected across all the most perilous places, to which the visitor may firmly cling, while the mad waters are driven in his face. I descended this foaming, roaring abyss, with feelings of indescribable awe. The louder than ten-thousand-thunder music of dread Niagara roared with the rolling waters from the hights above. Sometimes, as I journeyed downward into the gulfs of spray, the wind and water would dash in my face, almost beating my breath away, and threatening to hurl me from the rocky pathway to the fearful depths below! Then a flash of sunlight would dart through the spray, revealing rainbows of beauty and brilliance beyond the power of description. To the right were the dark and rugged rocks—to the left the snow-white torrents of Niagara's mighty river, rolling overward to the gulf beneath our feet.

I was informed by the guide, after we came out from the Cave, that but few have the nerve to pass under the Fall. Occasionally ladies have gone through. Indeed, thrilling as is the experience, I remember it as one of peculiar interest. It makes an impression upon the soul never to be forgotten.

> "What august scenes salute the wondering eye!
> Floods that seem gushing through unriven sky,
> Plunge madly down from glory into gloom—
> Flash up into spray, and thunder from the tomb;
> And with a fair, ascending wall of waves,
> Bow the broad stream, and veil its misty caves,
> While radiant splendors beautify the fall,
> And echoes, answering to the Cataract's call,
> Leap like living thought from rock to rock—
> Shadow of sound, and daughter of the shock."

I left the Falls of Niagara on the New York Central Railroad, *via* Lewiston, seven miles down the Niagara River, on the American side. Lewiston is an old town, rather dilapidated in appearance, and is located at the head of Navigation on the *lower* Niagara. From the Falls to this place, the river is deep and rapid; the banks are high, rocky, and abrupt; indeed, the scenery here is wildly picturesque. Above the Falls, the Niagara is wide and smooth, with low banks and grassy shores. Below, the river is turbulent and narrow; the foaming waters lash the rocks on either side with the greatest fury, roaring downwards, with the voice of many thunders.

From the depot at Lewiston, travelers are conveyed to the steamboat landing in omnibuses; and there was considerable competition among the different steamboat and railroad lines; it was really annoying to hear the loud askings and earnest urgings of the penny-a-word runners that infested all possible stopping places on the route.

At Lewiston, a magnificent lake-steamer was already lying to, waiting for travelers, and there was a large number in our company. As soon as the passengers and baggage were transferred from the depot to the steamer, our noble vessel headed downward toward Lake Ontario. While the passengers were going on board, I was amused at an old colored man, standing in our way, with a basket filled with half-ripe apples and dwarfed cherries, crying out lustily and good-humoredly, " Gemmen and ladies, business fuss, den pleasure—heer's de good apples—heer's de ripe cherries, heer's boaf—now come right 'long up to de basket, like *men*. If dese wasn't good for ye, de Lor' wouldn't have sent 'em to ye—*jist in this 'ticlar time to get 'em*—ONLY cent apiece, for gelorious fruit." Then turning politely to a gentleman at his side, who seemed to eye the tempting fruit with a little curiousness, our salesman, in a tender, winning voice, said most prettily, " Have some, sah?—dey's so 'licious!"

Soon we were afloat on Lake Ontario; but I should not forget to note Fort Niagara, at the mouth of Niagara River, on the American side. This fort presents a formidable front, looks well from the river and lake, and is distinguished in the historical associations of our country.

The first stopping place is Toronto, on the north side of the lake, the capital of the Canadas, situated thirty-six miles from the mouth of Niagara River. It was incorporated as a city in 1834, and now numbers 50,000 inhabitants. It is the seat of three colleges and numerous schools. The Parliament House, Governor's residence, the Colleges, Osgood Hall, the Banks, the Custom House, and Lunatic Asylum are among the prominent buildings. The site of the city is very beautiful, rising gradually from the water's edge. The scenery about the commodious harbor here, displays life and energy, and indicates the various commercial avocations of the people.

Leaving Toronto at sundown, the steamer passed out to the lake and into the night, so that all terrestrial things were soon invisible. There was an excellent piano on board, and a skillful, little French Canadian to use it. It added greatly to our enjoyment to have music's influence and power to cheer us over the waters.

Very early in the morning, a stiff south-easter rolled the vessel to and fro, very much to the discomfort of the few who were so soon out of bed. They could neither sit, stand, nor lie—only fall down, and get half way up, to be pitched about miscellaneously. Quite a number of the passengers were sea-sick—some slovenly fellows on the lower deck, vomiting and swearing alternately!

At daylight, we entered the great St. Lawrence. Who has not heard of the "Thousand Islands?" Their grandeur can not be described. Indeed, the eye sees here a mingling of the grand and gentle—the romantic and the picturesque. On either side, before, and behind, are innumerable islands, covered with foliage drooping down to the water, the overhanging boughs moving gracefully to and fro, as they are washed by the current. Some few of these islands are composed of solid rock, overgrown with fine moss; some present abrupt sides of rock, gray and flinty, while grass and shrubbery grow luxuriantly over their tops. The steamer seemed to be in a wilderness of woods, with a hundred rivers spreading outward like paths of shining silver on every side. Here and there was seen a fisherman, as his canoe glided

"Now she plows headlong through a ridge of troubled waters, and now trembles in a trough of flashing foam." Page 141.

silently along the waters, then was gone behind the leaves.

But the most exciting feature of a trip down the St. Lawrence is to pass over the famous "Rapids." The great rapids are Long Sault, the Coteau, the Cedars, the Cascades, and the Lachine.

The first of these is really thrilling to behold. The highest waves rise in the Lost or North channel. The sublime excitement of "*shooting them*," is greatly hightened by contrast. Before you reach them there is scarcely a breath of air stirring; every thing is calm and quiet, and the steamer glides as noiselessly and gently down the river, as if it were on the bosom of our own beautiful Ohio. Suddenly she enters a narrow channel, the waters of which are swift as arrows, yet she dashes through them in her lightning-way, and spurns the countless whirlpools beneath her. Forward, and close on either side are rocks, and precipices of water, and pyramidal breakers tossed high into the air. How shall we avoid being wrecked in that 'boiling abyss? But quick as thought, our obedient steamer mounts the wall of the waves and foam like a bird—now she ploughs headlong through a ridge of troubled waters, and now trembles in a trough of flashing foam, strikes a contending wave again so violently that sheets of water glance to the upper deck, then lands you a moment afterwards adown the calm, unruffled river!

When within thirty miles of Montreal, the high mountain from which the city takes its name appears in view. It is a *real mount*—a *Mont-real*, and no mistake. An hour's steaming more, and the evening shades gather everywhere, but not so densely as to hide from the gaze of the wondering traveler that stupendous structure, Victoria Bridge, an everlasting piece of masonry and wrought-iron, spanning the broad St. Lawrence at Montreal. The bridge is *nearly two miles long*, and stands on twenty-five substantial pillars of stone. The superstructure is of iron—not a stick of timber is in the entire bridge! But the narrow streets and tall palaces of the city are at hand!

At nightfall our faithful steamer is safely moored to one of the magnificent piers of the city wharf, and I step into an omnibus for the hotel.

On Sabbath morning, at eight o'clock, I was delighted with a merry chime of church-bells rung from the Catholic Cathedral, near our hotel. I had a curiosity to look inside of the largest church on the American Continent, and determined to go over and see it. Surely the architecture of this edifice is unequalled in strength, massiveness, and beauty. From the outside it looks like an immense, marble mountain, and the interior view reminds one of out-of-doors. I do not know the precise dimensions of this huge building, but am informed that eight thousand people can be comfortably seated within. The ceremonies of the service are peculiarly impressive, on account of the sweet sublimity of the music and organ.

I left this place of "unknown tongues" and unaccountable paraphernalia, and walked down street to an unpretending Protestant church, and entered there. I recognized a friend there with whom and his family I had made acquaintance on the steamer. Being early I passed the time in perusing a hymn-book that lay on the pew by my side. It was a collection used by the Baptist denomination. I was in a Baptist church. I felt to be "a stranger in a strange land," but experienced a precious comfort in these lines of a hymn upon which I happened to turn:—

> "Through this wide wilderness I roam,
> Far distant from my peaceful home;
> I faint with toil, and often say,
> Let not thy chariot long delay.
>
> As one forsaken and forlorn,
> Thy absence, dearest Lord, I mourn,
> I long thy blissful face to see,
> And dwell for ever near to thee.'"

Perhaps this hymn touched me the more impressively, on account of my wanderings of spirit as well as of body. When one travels he needs to keep a constant watch upon his thoughts and words—he is apt to go astray from his best Friend. I remember passing the Sabbath nearly all in sorrow and loneliness. This is not the right state of mind. Sometimes we forget to perform our vows to love and serve our Master with faithfulness—and then we mourn. I am one of those who believe in a smiling, cheerful Christianity. When we are sad, our hearts are not safe and free. We need more zeal and earnestness than we are wont to exercise.

As soon as the minister announced the text, I felt more than ordinarily anxious to hear the sermon. The speaker appeared to be a good man—he wore the face of a Christian. "For Zion's sake will I not hold my peace, and for Jerusalem's sake will I not rest, until her righteousness goes forth as brightness." There is a sermon in the text alone; but the words spoken there that day, are among the treasured things of my heart.

The early morning train from Montreal brought me to St. Johns, distant twenty-one miles; from thence, fourteen miles farther, in a south-easterly course, I passed over a new branch of the same road, through bogs and tangled woods, to Farnham.

The surface of the country between St. Johns and Montreal is even and well cultivated. The wheat was just beginning to head; the oats were yet " as blades of grass." Great quantities of pease are raised in this country. I never saw so much pease in all my life in the States, as I saw in a single field here. Barley flourishes well in Canada. Indeed, the principal crops cultivated here are oats, pease, barley, and beans. To overlook the Queen's English of the couplet from an old song, its sentiment is not so far out of the way for states' men—I mean people of the U. S.—*us*.

> " You, nor I, nor nobody knows
> How oats, pease, beans, and barley *grows*."

To know all this, one must go to Canada and see.

St. Johns is a beautiful little city, located on the outlet of Lake Champlain. Numerous shade trees adorn the streets, and render the side-walks cool and pleasant.

Not much grading is required in the construction of a railroad in this part of Canada. The surface of the ground is level and sandy for the most part; yet there are some swamps of considerable size that need *corduroying* and ballasting, before the track can be laid down and kept in order. The new road seems smooth and solid. The ride through this section of country is romantic. Dark pine forests may be seen sometimes extending close alongside the track for miles, and reaching far outward to the low hills in the distance. Here and there we cross a meadow, and scent the fresh mown grass which the merry French harvesters are tossing to the winds to cure. Very often a "clearing" is in sight; forest trees with leaves withered and curled, for the woodman's ax has *deadened* the trees' life by hacking the fatal circle around their trunks; smoking log heaps; crackling, burning brush; new made rails; and the fresh, upturned soil ready to receive the mellowing light and heat of the sun.

One striking feature of this country is, that the public highways frequently lead directly through fields of growing grain, without a fence for guard. The law here requires that all pasture-field and line fences shall be kept in good repair, and that stock shall be kept in those pastures and not permitted to roam at large. It is curious to drive along these smooth, well-trodden thoroughfares, with the ripening grain bending over and touching the wheels of the carriage as we pass.

Stages run regularly from Farnham to neighboring towns and villages in every direction; one of these took me to Bedford. From thence I used my own conveyance—a safe one—and strolled along, at a raspberrying gait, to my destination for that day.

I should not forget to make mention of the numerous new school houses that dot the road-side all through this region of country. Most of them are comfortable brick buildings with steep roofs and small windows. Heavy snows fall here; hence the necessity for the first pecuharity. Perhaps the wonderful brilliancy of the young Canadian's bright, black eyes renders the profusion of sunlight unnecessary; hence the choice of small windows!

One day I had a grand drive for a circle of twenty miles, in company with a kind friend. We passed through several villages, and over some of the most delightful lands in Canada. A heartsome, healthful place is Frelighsburg, nestled down in a fertile valley, at the foot of the Pinnacle Mountain, in Missisquoi county. At noon, we drove up to a country mansion—a farm house—and called for dinner. After dinner some one proposed a ramble to the summit of Pinnacle Mountain, as it was in full view, and was a point of much visitation, on account of its beauty and sublimity. It seemed near by, but upon inquiry, I learned that it was full six miles off.

From want of time to go so far, the attempt was abandoned. From the summit of this mountain the traveler may, if the air is clear, get a bird's eye view of Montreal, the St. Lawrence—like a strip of tape away to the north;—Lake Champlain—seeming a bit of silver sparkling in the light;—the Green Mountains of Vermont—Lake Memphremagog—besides a number of towns and picturesque villages.

\* \* \* \* \* \* \* \* \* \*

Leaving the delightful and picturesque scenery of northern Vermont and southeastern Canada, I arrived at Montreal, on my return, about four o'clock in the afternoon. As soon as the steam ferry boat, *Iron Duke*, touched the piers of the city landing, the passengers were beset by a crowd of impertinent runners and cab-men, crying out lustily, " Cab, sir—cab, sir ;" "carriage, sir--ride, sir."

Mixed up in the gang of cab-men and drivers of divers vehicles, are a number of rowdy boys, intent on carrying somebody's baggage somewhere. It is really annoying to run the gantlet of these croaking fellows. "Av yer baggage carried, cap'n," said an overgrown seventeener to me, seizing hold of my valise, and well nigh dragging it from my hand. "Certainly, sir," said I, "but prefer carrying it myself, thank you."

But these askings became so numerous and loud, that I was compelled to abridge my reply to a firm "No, sir ;" and finally to a cross, decided." *No !*". Better than this, however, is to pretend deafness, and pay no attention whatever to these unmannerly pests of ports and depots.

Speaking of cabs, it occurs to me that it might be interesting to describe the kind in use in Montreal. They are nothing more nor less than two-story carts—box built, after the fashion of an omnibus, and painted green or some other color! The driver, as soon as he gets a passenger inside, perches himself on the top, high aloft of all surrounding movables, and is quickly out of the way and out of sight, hurrying along through the labyrinthine streets of the city.

These two-wheeled affairs are common among the French in Canada. The country cabs are quite rude and rough. Frequently, on the way between Vermont and Montreal, I met companies of Canadian harvesters, huddled together in a little cart, drawn by a pony of real value and beauty, journeying over to the States to find employment in the fields.

The haying time in Canada is in the month of July.

I noticed a vast amount of white daisies in the meadows, giving them the appearance of fields of white clover, or of buckwheat in blossom.

\* \* \* \* \* \* \*

To-day I am ascending the St. Lawrence, homeward bound. The rapids are overcome by means of canals and locks; therefore, our ascent of the river will be much slower than our descent over the rapids, at railroad speed. But I like this variety. Just now, I look out from the cabin window and see the river off to the right, foaming and writhing by the rocks and cedars. It is "Cedar Rapids." Our noble vessel is the same that proudly rode those swift billows a few days ago; but she chooses to pass them by on this return.

We are in a canal sixty feet wide, and deep enough for the largest steamers. The masonry at the locks is solid as the hills, and truly magnificent in its design and architecture. It surpasses any thing I have ever seen in the way of public improvements in the States. Now we come to a neat, wooden bridge thrown across the canal, within ten feet of the surface of the water, and, apparently, firmly resting on the abutments on either side. How shall we pass that? Soon as the query comes to the mind, a man who stands near the bridge presses a lever, and the bridge turns aside! The manœuvre is performed by water-power; a revolving waterwheel, somewhere beneath the abutments, turns the bridge away until we pass, then turns it back again. These gudgeon bridges are numerous along the canal.

It seems like traveling by steamboat overland! The fields are close to us, and the long water-grasses are brushed by the paddle-wheels on right and left as we pass along. Here is a railroad crossing, with the usual precaution on a high and prominent board resting on two upright posts:—

"Railroad crossing—look out for the engine."
"Traverse de chemin de fer."

So, a Frenchman who can not read a word of English, must *defer* when the train comes! Here is the only place that I have found where a warning *to* railroad trains might, with propriety, be signaled. While this bridge is turned, and the steamer is passing, there is a fit moment when even the iron-horse and all his riders might well afford to be careful, for should he rush heedlessly onward to this cut-off, he would surely *defer* his race, and with battered bones and unjointed frame his last spark of life would be quenched in the waters.

The flowers are out in their loveliest attire in the gardens that abound on the canal-side. What so pleasing as this! to stand upon the deck and admire them as we glide along—new ones presenting their bright colors and fragrant odors every moment. And the overhanging trees afford us the cool shade of their leafy boughs, while the sweet tones of a guitar, touched by skillful fingers, greet our ears from the cabin of our floating home. But the flowers are dearest of all. A friend, not long since, spoke of the flowers, and called them "God's smiles." And so they are:—

So spake a gentle friend,
And in her meek simplicity, expressed a truth,
Of meaning full and sweet, as from above,
Came to the mind of him, who, pen-inspired,
Wrote, "God is love."

> Flowers are God's smiles,—
> Who doubts it for a moment? come and see
> The blooming, fragrant, variegated bed,
> So beautiful and gay, and each one smiling,
> As if it said—
>
> For you we live and smile;
> For you we bend, and bloom, and clothe ourselves,
> With colors manifold, all bright and fair;
> We fill your rooms with sweetness; our odors
> Float through the air.
>
> Flowers are God's smiles—
> Carnations ever new, tall Hollyhocks,
> Creeping Verbenas, drooping Fuchias,
> Dahlias stately, Roses pure, and Lilies say—
> God smiles in us.
>
> In the better land,
> Will flowers adorn the city's golden streets?
> I can not say; but while I linger here—
> Sweet flowers! I'll love them, for there to usward
> God's smiles appear!

But, kind reader, you will weary with this ramble, I fear. Not that you do not love flowers, but that you dislike these pen-wanderings. And as I have been so dreamy this sultry summer's day, I ask pardon for this, and promise to write from Canada no more.

# TO A DEPARTED MOTHER.

My mother, dearest, thou art gone,
   For thee there falls the streaming tear;
Though thou canst not to me return,
   I claim thee present with me here:
       I can not tell
       How long, how well,
I loved thee, O, my mother dear!

I know thou'rt gone to angel-land,
   And that thou ever lovest me—
Thy poor, lone child; come, take my hand,
   And let me go and stay with thee!
       For, mother, thou
       Art happy now,
And I thy happiness would see.

But weary days or tedious years
   May vail from me thy Paradise;
Yet I can look through sorrow's tears
   To glorious things beyond the skies!
       My soul goes there
       On wings of prayer,
Then skyward, too, my hopes arise.

Then, wherefore should my soul be stirred?
"THEY SHALL FIND REST THAT LEARN OF ME;"
I'll take thee, Saviour, at Thy word,
   And humbly pray that I may be
      Prepared by grace
      To see Thy face,
And find eternal rest in Thee.

# VISIT TO THE MAMMOTH CAVE.

I MADE the acquaintance of a clever young Ohioan, at Louisville, Ky., and in his agreeable company, started for the Mammoth Cave on a beautiful afternoon in October. The cars on the Louisville and Nashville Railroad took us to Woodland Station, where we arrived at eight o'clock at night, distant eleven miles from the Cave. Evening closed over us as we sped along our iron way, and a dark, cloudy night followed. The bright up-flashings of the lightning occasionally lifted the dense darkness away, revealing to us the outlines of the distant hills, and the location of many snug farm houses on either side of the way; while the distant thunder and the sobbing of the rain storm were blended with the roaring of the train.

From Woodland, early the next morning, we started afoot, over a barren, uncultivated woodland, toward the Cave. The road lies through an unbroken forest of scrubby trees, and over sandy hills, until it leads the traveler to the vicinity of the Cave, where the scenery is more cheering. Just as we entered the wood, a guide board reminded us that we were fairly started

"FOR. MAT CAVE, ☞"

Our pedestrian journey was pleasant, and at noon we

were eating dinner at the Cave Hotel. After dinner we strolled down the hillside to the entrance of the Cave, and along the banks of Green River, enjoying Nature in her autumn solitudes and quiet teachings.

Next morning a large company had assembled at the Hotel—some from Cincinnati, others from Philadelphia, and three from Cuba—all ready to explore the Cave, under the care of "Mat," an experienced guide. At nine o'clock, each, with lamp "trimmed and burning," in company entered the subterranean world. The entrance to the Cave is one hundred and ninety-four feet above the level of Green River; it is about twenty-five feet high, thirty wide; and at all seasons a mist or fog may be seen at the entrance.

The Mammoth Cave breathes once a year. In summer, when the temperature of external air is above that of the Cave, the current sets outward. The Cave is all summer exhaling a single breath. When this order is reversed, the Cave makes an inspiration—takes in a breath—all the long winter. When the outer and inner temperature are the same, the Cave ceases to breathe—holds its breath. Hence, in spring and autumn, there is no motion of air at the mouth of the Cave.

A change of seasons is unknown in the Cave. Day and night, morning and evening have no existence there. There is an eternal summer, a deep and almost painful silence, the like of which has no parallel. The atmosphere of the Cave, owing to its peculiar chemical qualities, is remarkably pure and bracing. A journey of nine miles among its labyrinths is less fatiguing than one of three miles out above.

The first object of interest is the Rotunda, the ceiling

of which is one hundred feet high, and its greatest diameter is one hundred and seventy-five feet. The floor of the Rotunda is strewn with vats, water pipes, and other materials used by the saltpetre miners in 1812. The wood of which they are made shows no signs of decay.

Audobon's Avenue leads off from the Rotunda one and a half miles to a collection of stalactites. I noticed innumerable bats flitting about and clinging to the rocky walls there. A little further on, we came to the Methodist Church, eighty feet in diameter, built of rocks. A shelf of rock forms the pulpit, and here the Gospel was expounded more than fifty years ago.

Passing onward, the Giant's Coffin appears. This is a huge rock, forty feet long, twenty feet wide, and eight in depth, and from the point where we viewed it, presents a striking resemblance to a coffin. Right over the Giant's Coffin, on the ceiling, is the figure of an Anteater. This picture is composed of black gypsum, and rests upon a background of white lime-stone.

A short distance beyond the Giant's Coffin, in the Main Cave, a group of figures in a sitting posture, represents a Giant, Wife, and Child.

Leaving all the wonderful sights, we pass on hastily through the Deserted Chamber, the Wooden Bowl Cave, Martha's Palace, Minerva's Dome, Bottomless Pit, Reveler's Hall, Scotchman's Trap, Fat Man's Misery, (a narrow, low and very crooked fissure in the rock, extending for a distance of half a mile, through which none but a slender, little man can pass comfortably,) on to River Hall and Bacon Chamber.

The next thing that attracts especial attention is the Dead Sea, the River Styx, and the Natural Bridge.

Approaching the shore of Echo River, we passed the Dead Sea and the river Styx. A high, rocky path leads around one side of the sea, some sixty feet above the surface of the water, leaving its mysterious depths, its gloomy gulfs and its silent shores, deep down on the left.

Here is one of the most dangerous passages in the Cave. The pathway leads among rugged rocks that overhang the sea; now turns suddenly to the right; now winds down a deep declivity of slippery clay, and now crosses a deep, wide chasm, on a slender wooden bridge, from which some one of the party drops a pebble, while we all listen to its fall, as it glances and bounds from rock to rock, until at last it *chugs* into the watery abyss far below.

Down, down we grope, each with lamp in one hand, and holding with the other, as step by step we descend to the rough ledges of the rock, or to the rude railing of iron, until we reach the water's edge. Here we find two small boats, built in the Cave expressly for ferrying the river Styx at this place. Our guide, and his assistant, Pat, who has charge of the basket of provisions for dinner, soon row us across the river.

Now we shall have a long, tedious walk over the wet sand, and that accomplished, we reach the wildly romantic Echo River.

Here we find two boats ready to take our company on board. As the party is large, we divide, giving the ladies and their attendants the larger and more comfortable boat, and the more experienced guide, while the rest of us put ourselves in care of Pat, the Irishman, who knows better how to carry the dinner and make droll jokes, than to pilot a boat. However, Pat is willing to try his hand at the oars, and we are all ready.

Now comes a scene beyond description. The passengers in the forward boat have nicely arranged their lamps in a row on either side of their vessel, and she floats away. Soon we follow on. The lamp-lights gleam out brilliantly over the crystal river, revealing the black, rocky river-shores and the low sky of stone above. The water is so clear and transparent that we can easily discern the shining sands on the river-bed many feet beneath. The boat seems a fairy thing gliding noiselessly away in air!

Listen! Some one of the advance boat's company is singing:—

> "He made him a boat of birchen bark,
> Which carried him off from the shore;
> Long he followed that meteor spark,—
> The wind was high, *and the night was dark,*
> And the boat returned no more."

Now, all is silent as the grave! The oarsmen have heard that touching melody, and they rest on their oars. Hark! they come—the echoes! Afar down the river they linger in the caverns; now they are wafted back to us; faintly, sweetly, softly, they say,

> "The boat returned no more."

Never was human voice so angel-toned—never so plaintive as the lingering, dying echo,

> "The boat returned no more,"

As soon as the last gentle echoes are hushed away in the dark silence, the advance boat, now far ahead, glides quickly away from our view in a short curve in the river, and all is dense darkness before. Yet the fair singer's voice we hear:

> "And oft from the Indian hunter's camp,
> This lover and maid so true,
> Are seen at the hour of midnight damp,
> To cross the lake by their firefly lamp,
> And to paddle their light canoe."

All the return the fairies utter, comes from afar off, but the words are thrice repeated:

> "To paddle their light canoe,"—
> ——— "their light canoe,"
> ——————— "canoe."

\*  \*  \*  \*

While the advance party were so richly enjoying their voyage, our boat was slowly falling behind, on account of Pat's awkwardness at the oars. Sometimes we were jammed unceremoniously against the rocky river-shore; again we were piloted along where the water was within two or three feet of skull-bumping rocks above; and unless we had bowed low, our heads would have been scratched worse than ever was a puzzled school-boy's.

All this time, Pat was earnest and industrious, yet every motion he gave the boat was exactly the motion he didn't intend to give it, and he attributed the zigzags and wabblings of the frail craft, to its contrariness!

"An' now d'ye see this!" would be his expression, every time his own left-handed and no-headed philosophy would carry the boat 'ker-buff against a rock!

"Whin iver I howld her aboot—ye see the conthrary owld plague goes over fornenst me, jist. Will ye's, Misthers, be afther sayten yer-selves fornenst me, wid yer faces before ye's, till I get the owld tub out of this botherin wather?"

After some protracted and animated debating, tending almost to "mutiny and war," we at length prevailed on Pat to row *straight ahead*, and we would do the piloting ourselves. With this understanding my friend and I took the rudder in hand and succeeded in guiding the boat, not where the *water* seemed to be deepest, but where the *air* was deepest between our heads and the overhanging rocks.

We voyaged on this remarkable river for about one mile, admiring the placid waters that were never ruffled into waves by the winds of heaven; waters that are always clear and pure, though ever flowing through darkness and gloom, teaching a lesson of purity and innocence to every adventurous explorer, whose lot is cast in the outer world, all dark and desolate with sin.

Leaving Echo River and its charms behind, we enter Silliman's Avenue—a long and pebbly lane, about three miles in extent. On a wide, flat rock in this avenue, Pat unbasketed and arranged, in genuine rural style, our dinner, which consisted of roast turkey, bread, butter, fruit, pies, etc., all of which were disposed of without delay or outer-world delicacy. Our beverage was the cold, bright, sparkling water that gushed from the side of the Cave within a few feet of our table.

Dinner over, we were all rested and refreshed; then hurried on toward the end of the "Long Route." We passed some narrow, winding passages; climbed several steep and closely walled stairways and ladders of rock; descended a number of deep and dismal declivities, until we arrived at Snow Ball Chamber. This is an immense room, about eighty feet in width and three hundred in length, with a decorated ceiling of white flowers and snow-balls of gypsum, a little above the hand's reach.

Here we spent a half hour in wonder and admiration. Never, in all the palaces that human hands have erected, was there so much grandeur, or such exquisite ornaments!

After gathering a few specimens of this singular and beautiful formation, we took a democratic method of deciding when we should return. The majority decided that we should at once retrace our steps from this point, although some of us complied rather reluctantly with the decision.

Soon we were on our way back to the entrance of the Cave. Our outward journey was not void of interest, or without many new discoveries and delights. But we hasten out to the world. After journeying *under* land and *over* water for about eight miles, the air becomes cooler. We are near the mouth of the Cave. Now a fresh breeze is blowing in our faces. Our lights are extinguished by its force, but we shall need them no longer, for the moon and the stars are shining in the high-off heavens, and we are but a few rods from the hotel where supper and sleep shall fit us for new adventures on tomorrow.

All in all, my trip to the Mammoth Cave was a pleasant and profitable one; one that I shall never regret nor forget. Truly, the works of God are sublime and awe-inspiring everywhere. At Niagara, His mighty power is told in perpetual thunders,—at the Mammoth Cave, in the no less impressiveness of a silence that can be felt.

## MY EARLY HOME.

Love, Peace, and Repose! the tenderest trio
    Of musical words ever blended in one—
That one word is *Home*—'mid the hills of Ohio—
    Dear home of my childhood in years that are gone.

There, father and mother, two sisters, one brother,
    With hopes, like their hearts, united, abide;
Their treasures in this world are few; in another,
    A heritage holy and glory beside.

In fancy I wander, this sweet summer morning,
    Away to the wheat-field, just over the hill;
'Tis harvest-time now, and the reapers are coming
    To gather the waiting grain, goldened and still.

Many harvests have passed, many summers have ended,
    Since here I oft toiled, with glad reapers, before,
And felt the great bounty of Heaven extended,
    Giving joy to the worker, and bread to the poor.

Long ago, I remember, when, thirsty and tiring,
    The harvesters came to the old maple shade,
How they quaffed the pure water, so cool and inspiring,
    That gushed from the fountain that Nature had made.

And I think of the orchard, and the apples that yellowed,
    Half hidden by leaves in the "big early tree :"
Ah, the apples, how luscious, when ripened and mellowed,
    Then dropped in the clover for sisters and me!

Old home of my youth, so humble, so cherished,
    Thy hallowéd memory cheers me to-day;
When all other thoughts of the past shall have perished,
    Remembrance of thee shall illumine my way.

Sweet home in Ohio, now farewell for ever!
    I've wandered afar from thy dear cottage door:
I'll visit thee, love thee; but never, oh, never,
    Will thy charms, or my childhood, return any more.

# VISIT TO KENTUCKY.

Toward the close of the fair month of May, we started on a short summer tour among the homes and schools of Kentucky and Tennessee. Our way led us over the Pennsylvania Central Railroad, amid its thousand picturesque scenes, and its unrivaled comforts and conveniences to the traveler.

Tourists will be repaid a hundred fold by passing this way, among the rich farms of Eastern Pennsylvania, along the romantic Susquehanna, the winding valley of the "Blue Juniata;" and then to climb the lofty Alleghany Mountains by steam, and on and away over the western slope, down the wild Conemaugh, until the beautiful Ohio appears beyond the smoke and dust of the Iron City, is truly grand!

From Pittsburgh's noise and soot we continued our journey westward, over the prompt and well managed Fort Wayne and Chicago extension of the great Central Railroad; loitering a day or two at the dear old homestead among the hills of Ohio, with father, mother, sisters, brother, where in days gone by, we so often mingled our voices, our hopes, our fears, and our loves. What sacred memories associate with

"The orchard, the meadow, the deep-tangled wild wood,
And every loved spot which our infancy knew!"

But those days of endearing union and communion as an unbroken family, when all our aims were one, when the same humble cabin-roof sheltered us every one from all the outer world's storm and strife; when the only center and charm of each life were blended in the sweet thought of home—those happy days have fled for ever! Yet the privilege of meeting, even seldom, now, with the "loved ones at home," to talk of our varied pursuits and prospects in the world, and to join hearts in the one cherished hope of a Home in Heaven at last, makes it a joyous time for us all together.

There is not much time for observation while hurrying along by steam over hill and dale, valley, plain, and broad prairie; and three days of this journeying onward,

"Singing through the forest,
Rattling over bridges,
Shooting under arches,
Running over ridges,"

brought us, by way of Chicago, Lafayette, and Louisville, to the quaint and quiet little city of Frankfort, the capital of Kentucky.

During our stay in Frankfort we enjoyed the company of the children at a grand pic-nic, close by a cool, gushing spring, whose pure waters leap from the rock-side beneath the shade of ancestral elms and sycamores, near the banks of the Kentucky River.

From eight o'clock in the morning until six in the evening, the old woods rang with music and with mirth, out-springing from the hearts of hundreds of exultant children. The ample and delicious dinner brought in baskets, and eaten from a table of grass, the bright, sparkling water from the spring, the songs, the plays, the speeches, the jokes, the frolic, and the fun, all—

"As free, as free as the winds they were!"

And not until the far-reaching shadows of evening had gathered the silvery ripples from the surface of the river, and hushed to silence the warblings of the birds around, did we turn our faces homeward. That was, indeed, a jubilant day, and never shall its delights be forgotten. But the heart may not always be glad. There are times of pensive sorrow, and in the evening of our gala day, the hours brought silent and solemn lessons, when in company with a few young friends, we visited the Cemetery at Frankfort, by moonlight. It was a calm, sweet summer's evening, such as would inspire any soul with purest emotions.

The location of the Cemetery is on the summit of a hill that rises abruptly from the right bank of the Kentucky River, close above the town. The entire bluff, from the river shore to the summit, is densely covered with trees, bushes, and vines, forming an almost perpendicular mountain-wall of foliage. Within the enclosure, nature and art have blended their handiwork to form a most lovely resting place for the dead. White monuments of the purest marble rise up among evergreens, shrubs, and flowers!

The pale moonbeams shone downward through the darkened leaves, and touched, in quiet tenderness, the placid waters of the river far below; they lingered in loving nearness to the smooth white head-stones, here and there; but they seemed to rest more gently upon the little green graves under the cedars. Oh, the moonbeams were angel smiles! the zephyrs of night were angel-whispers, breathing holy vespers over the graves of loved ones sweetly sleeping!

Near the edge of this garden of graves, and overlooking the clear-flowing river below, is the grave of Daniel Boone. His only monument is an appropriate surrounding of rocks and forest trees, so arranged by art as to represent the wildness of an unbroken wilderness.

While we stood beside this grave and looked away up toward the full moon, we could see the topmost boughs of the tall firs and cedars waving to and fro very gently —stirred by the soft airs of summer night. It was a tender but touching symbol of life—Eternal Life; for the *living* branches waved, and their leaves were *evergreen!*

Rest on, thou honored slumberer in the tomb! Thy life was one of care and of conflict. For these hills and valleys, now the homes of the thousands who revere thy memory, were once "the dark and bloody ground." And when we all shall have slept like thee for a short night beneath the clay, may we rise to a fairer land above, where no savage foes molest or make afraid!

We made a second visit to the Cemetery, on a Sabbath afternoon, in the company of a kind friend, and his beloved children, (whose peaceful home was ours while we were at Frankfort,) and were more than ever impressed with the surprising beauty of the place. It speaks for the finer feelings of the people to see such adornment in these streets and walks, and around the dwellings of the inhabitants of the sad and silent city on the hill.

Never, in all our travels, have we received more genuine kindness and good cheer, than from the hands and hearts of the Kentuckians. The stranger is at home wherever he may chance to wander in their midst. And to any one who goes among them as a friend, and with an honest purpose, the most hearty welcome will be extended.

## AN ACROSTIC FOR ADELA.

Fair Adela, treasured jewel
Of the hearts that love thee best,
Rest for weary, waiting pilgrims,
Thou, with songs, hast cheered and blest.
Happy child, thy voice is ringing
In the morn, at noon, and night,
Singing sweetly—ever singing
Notes of love and dear delight.
Angels pause, with wings scarce lifted,
Moving round in airy tread,
Ever list'ning, watching, smiling—
Always near thee companied.
Dear Adela, yet remember,
Ere thy singing days are o'er,
Lo! there dawns a sweet "for ever,"
And a morning evermore!
May the Music of the angels,
Floating earthward through the air,
In the early breath of morning,
New life to thy spirit bear!
Days on earth shall thus be blissful—
Life, the earnest of the soul's
Everlasting rest in heaven,
Yielding peace and joy untold!

# A SUMMER RAMBLE.

From childhood we had a desire to see the nation's Capital; but never, until a leisure week in the middle of May, 1860, was an opportunity presented of gratifying that wish. In the cheerful company of a dear friend and relative from Ohio, Mr. W——, we left the Friendly City on the twelve o'clock, M. train, over the Philadelphia, Wilmington, and Baltimore Railroad, and reached Baltimore at four o'clock in the afternoon. The scenery along this road is pleasing in early summer-time, when the rich, half-opened clover blossoms redden the fields, and when the air is all fragrant with the health of growing leaves and sweet meadows spread in verdure fair and free!

As we gazed in silent admiration toward woodland, field, and hill upon the right, or toward the clear-flowing Delaware upon the left, our friend quoted very appropriately the words of the poet, Stennett:

> "Sweet fields arrayed in living green,
> And rivers of delight!"

What lessons are written on the forest leaves, on the blades of grass, and on the tender flowers! Nature's teachings are pure and peaceful; the more we study her truths, the more useful and happy we may be, because the Great Creator is revealed in every work that his hands have made. The more we learn from Nature, the more *natural* will be our conversation and our conduct. Why should we confine ourselves, or the little children, to books alone, trying to derive good by poring over dry paper and dead words all the summer day, while living, breathing, ever-bountiful Nature is spread out before us to bless us by her smiles and enrich us by her treasures?

Baltimore stands on an uneven surface, and commands a fine view of the Chesapeake Bay. The best view of the city we obtained from the summit of Washington Monument. This structure was erected by the state of Maryland in honor of the name it bears. It stands at the intersection of two beautiful squares adorned by rows of shade trees, fountains, and flowers. The corner-stone was laid on the Fourth of July, 1815. It is built on an eminence of one hundred feet above the tide, and consists of a square base of fifty feet by twenty-four in hight, surmounted by a column; the entire altitude, including the statue, is one hundred and eighty feet. Twelve steps lead us from the outer circle to the main entrance. The stairway winds up a dark, spiral passage in the interior of the main column, to the summit; but with the aid of a lantern, and by patient climbing, we reached the top in a few minutes.

And here we were repaid a thousand fold for the fatigue of reaching the place, for the whole city lay spread out in magnificent grandeur beneath. The visitor looks down and grows dizzy at the sight, and intuitively recoils at the thought of falling. Human beings appear no larger than grasshoppers, and horses and wagons than little toys! It all seems to be a picture, only you behold the bustle and stir of life, and hear the hum of a busy, toiling multitude below you. These are features that can not be painted. And then the neat cottages, the palatial residences, the orchards and the gardens round about the edges of the city, added a charm to the entire scene, such as impresses the mind with a sense of the truly beautiful.

But the many objects of interest in the city and vicinity are so varied and admirable, that we reluctantly turn from them even to the no less pleasing associations connected with the Public Schools of the city. Reading is particularly regarded in the higher schools of Baltimore. We heard one of the pupils in the Western Female High School read Poe's "Raven," with a feeling and pathos, such as few professed elocutionists can employ. And speaking of that unhappy poet, Poe, leads us to say that his grave is very near to the very school above mentioned. We procured the key to the cemetery where Poe is buried, and rambled alone for a while among the tombs. There are several graves right under the church, shut out from sunlight, all dusty, drear, and lone. As we groped our way among these vaults and tombs, in the darkness and silence, we at length stumbled upon the forsaken grave of Edgar Allen Poe! Strange appropriateness! that a life so sad and forsaken should lay its clay in this dark slumber, away from flowers, away from friends, away from the returning light of day and the dews of evening, that, blended, bring forget-me-nots to blossom upon the graves of loved ones departed. While we tarried alone in the sad, shadowy twilight over the neglected grave of Poe, his own wild words were not an unfit expression of our silent musings:

> "Deep into that darkness peering,
>     Long I stood there, wondering, fearing,
> Doubting, dreaming dreams no mortal
>     Ever dared to dream before;
> But the silence was unbroken,
> And the darkness gave no token,
> And the only word there spoken
>     Was the whispered word, 'Lenore!'
> This *I* whispered, and an echo
>     Murmured back the word 'Lenore!'
> Merely this, and nothing more."

But we must haste away from a thousand objects of interest and have a day's stroll in Washington City. Of course, the experience of Parson Brownlow will not apply to all who visit the nation's Capital. The parson says, that, when he approached the City of Washington, he felt an unusual influence at work upon him, and on questioning his fellow-travelers, he found that many others were affected in the same manner. He attributed it to some strange atmospheric phenomenon, unaccountable, and exceedingly well calculated to lead its victims into disgrace and trouble. He says, this singular sensation made him *feel like stealing any thing and every thing within his reach!* Surely there must be a wonderful enchantment round about the Capital City!

Washington has been called the "City of Magnificent Distances," and it well merits the name. The streets are wide and airy, and ornamented with shade trees; the yards and gardens are tastefully decorated with shrubs and flowers. Shade trees are brain trees. Fruit trees are stomach trees. Judging by a rule like this, there are more brains than stomachs in Washington; but the trees were not planted by Congressmen, hence the result may be different about the Capitol itself!

The Smithsonian Institute is named after its founder, James Smithson, and will honorably perpetuate the name. The edifice is built of red sand-stone, and is 447 feet in length by 160 in breadth. We spent the best part of our visit here, and wished for a week more time to study the various objects of interest presented. There are specimens of almost every known animal, bird, fish, reptile, and insect; rich paintings; relics; mummies; philosophical and astronomical apparatus, &c., &c.; and each item is a lesson in itself.

The surroundings of Washington are beautiful in the extreme. The lovely Potomac bearing off toward the sea; the low range of hills on every side; and then the glory, and the life, and the fragrance of the sweet month of May, added charms to the city and cheered our sojourn all the while.

## THE MAY TIME.

'Tis beautiful May morning,
  My life is glad and free,
And many playful voices
  Are calling unto me,
To wander 'mid the blossoms,
  And breathe the honeyed air,—
To roam across the meadows
  Among the lilies fair.

To some secluded valley,
  Adorned by flowers of May,
Or far to forest wild-wood,
  Oh let me haste away!
Where bright the streamlet bubbles
  O'er beds of moss and sand,
And where the warbling song birds
  Sing of the fairy-land.

Beside the sparkling river—
  Whose faithful mirror-breast
Reflects a thousand beauties—
  Shall be my noon-day rest.

## THE MAY TIME.

My soul is here delighted
  With the loveliness I see,
And I bless my gracious Father
  For his tenderness to me.

And when the twilight lingers
  Along the river shore,
I'll think of life's calm evening,
  When all our toils are o'er;
I'll think of coming day-dawn,
  In the heavenly land above,
Where we'll share the blissful sunlight
  Of a Saviour's ceaseless love!

## UP THE HUDSON.

On a pleasant evening, about the middle of July, we took passage from New York city on a magnificent steamer bound for a sight-seeing expedition up the Hudson. There were several hundred passengers on board, all happy and hopeful as children, for it was a time of joy, and it would have made a miser glad to spend his dollar in such company, and amid so many buoyant anticipations.

As the noble vessel moved out from the pier into the waters of the Hudson, and glided noiselessly northward, leaving the crowded city behind, and gathering in the refreshing airs of summer evening that were playing to and fro along the river-shores, it seemed a floating paradise! Here and there, as we sped along, a salute was fired from the shore by friends of the steamer, and a welcoming response rang out from her bell, echoing among the hills around.

Soon we approached the Palisades on the west bank, standing between water and sky like immense walls of fluted rock. The shades of evening hung darkly around their base and far out upon the river, while the setting sun threw a crown of golden light on their summits, coronating their very abruptnesses with kingly grandeur and sublimity. We tarried long on the upper deck, watching the picturesque palisades, until the night shadows were let down to obscure them all from our gaze. Then, when we could no longer behold the far-off hills, we fancied we could see the farm-houses on the hill-sides among the distant Highlands, the weary harvesters resting around their cottage doors, and the little children listening to the harvest-tales! And these dreamy fancies soon wooed us away to "sure-enough" dreams in our comfortable berth, where we rested until the early dawn of the morrow awoke us to look about in Albany.

Wishing to see the Hudson River and its belongings in broad day-light, we took the morning boat for Newburg, and enjoyed a down river voyage, admiring the scenery as it every moment presented new and living pictures; no, smiling, breathing *realities*, too exquisitely beautiful to be pictured by pen or pencil—the fields of ripened wheat; the clovered plains; the green meadows; the fruitful orchards; the leafy groves, all waving in the brilliant sun-light; the snug cottages, nestled cosily among the little hills or down in the shady valleys; the ten thousand charms of the ever-glorious country gladdening the eye and heart of every beholder!

\*　　　\*　　　\*　　　\*　　　\*　　　\*

Choosing a young companion from the Academy, at Newburg, we left the town, and were soon along the river-side, afoot, on our way to Idlewild, four miles below. This romantic spot, once an *idle wild*, has become, by the hand of genius and industry, the lovely retreat of one of the world's most gifted sons. Who has not heard of Nathaniel P. Willis, and who will not congratulate so great a favorite upon having this peaceful home, retired and beautiful, on the banks of the Hudson?

Mr. and Mrs. Willis gave us a cheerful welcome to Idlewild and its rural surroundings, and permitted their own sweet-hearted little daughters, Lillian and Edith. to ramble with us up the glen, then down to the meadows, out to the orchard, away to the raspberry fields; and we were as jolly a company as ever rollicked the glades and greens of Idlewild!

Now the children would gather flowers from the glenside and weave them into bouquets; now bring us a handful of luscious raspberries from the very edge of a precipice; and now off and away again like chamois over the moss-covered rocks; and then linger a moment and look back to laugh at our vain attempts to keep from blundering headlong over the bluffs and banks overhanging the cascade.

And so that summer's afternoon fled away too soon, leaving us less time to spend with the poet himself than we wished. Mr. Willis is a kind and genial man. Everybody loves him for his social good-humor and his winning conversational powers. You feel in the presence of a friend indeed, while in company with Mr. Willis, yet you know your companion who talks so pleasingly is one of the greatest of living authors. His mild, blue eye is full of poetry. We could easily believe ourselves in the immediate presence of the author of "Hagar in the Wilderness," "Absalom," "The Healing of the Leper," "Unwritten Music," and "Parrhasius."

Prominent among the many richly bound books that we observed on the table in Mr. Willis's study, and on the center table in the parlor at Idlewild, was the

"Old Family Bible." At once we thought of the familiar lines by George P. Morris, his associate editor and fraternal brother in the *Home Journal*, and the song, set to this sweet melody, breathed to our soul the tenderest tribute to the Blessed Book:

"This Book is all that's left me now,
　Tears will unbidden start;
With falt'ring lip and throbbing brow,
　I press it to my heart;
For many generations past,
　Here is our family tree,—
My mother's hands this Bible clasped,
　She, dying, gave it me.

"Ah! well do I remember those
　Whose names these records bear;
Who round the hearth-stone used to close,
　After the evening prayer—
And speak of what those pages said,
　In tones my heart would thrill!
Though they are with the silent dead,
　Here are they living still.

"My father read this holy Book,
　To brothers, sisters dear;
How calm was my poor mother's look,
　Who leaned God's word to hear!
Her angel face, I see it yet!
　What thronging memories come!
Again that little group is met
　Within the walls of home.

"Thou truest Friend man ever knew,
　Thy constancy I've tried;
Where all were false, I've found thee true,
　My Counsellor and Guide.
The mines of earth no treasures give
　That could this volume buy:
In teaching me the way to live,
　It taught me how to die."

But twilight came down upon the quiet Hudson and lingered around the mansion at Idlewild, and we bade adieu to our hospitable friends, and retraced our steps toward Newburg. Lillian and Edith accompanied us down the valley as far as "Pig-tight Gate," and there we parted from two of as dear little children as angels ever loved. After all the farewells had been said, their merry voices called after us,

> "Good-bye, good-bye,
> Hope to see you ere we die!"

Yes, God bless them a thousand times! We shall see them by-and-by, we trust, in the fairest, and loveliest, and heavenliest of homes!

## STANZAS.

*Memoria illorum haud facile transit.*

[ Lines written on hearing of the death of a young friend, who was called to rest only nine days subsequent to her father's decease. ]

It was our heavenly Father's will
Our cup of grief to doubly fill;
For quickly, from her crumbling clay,
Lucinda, too, has passed away!

Oh! why was she, in youthful bloom,
Called to the lonely, silent tomb?
How can our hearts, yet bleeding, say,
Lucinda, too, has passed away!

She faded—like the blushing rose
Whose brightest petals soonest close;
Or like a calm, sweet summer's day,
Lucinda, too, has passed away!

She did not with us long remain
To mourn a father's loss in vain,
But him to greet, without delay,
Lucinda, too, has passed away!

All clad in white, with harps in hand,
From heaven there came a sister-band

## STANZAS.

Of angels fair, who smiled to say,
"Lucinda, come, O, come away!"

A choir, attuned to Zion's Song,
Their melting symphonies prolong
In Heaven, and shout the joyful lay,
Lucinda, too, has come away!

We feel our two-fold sorrow here—
The heaving sigh—the burning tear;
Still, O, how glad we are to say,
They both in Christ have passed away!

## ON THE MOUNTAIN.

"Round Top" mountain, in York county, Pennsylvania, is a point well worth visiting. One lovely evening in September, our friend, Mr. H——, a teacher in Marietta, Pa., proposed a visit to its summit, and in half an hour we were ready for the excursion.

Procuring a little boat on the bank of the Susquehanna, we were soon afloat toward the opposite shore, from whence the tall mountain loomed up cloud-ward, foliaged from base to summit with maples, oaks, and evergreens.

The river is nearly a mile wide at Marietta, and from its placid surface, as we floated away, we obtained a magnificent view of the mountain side. The autumn leaves, not yet browned by the frosts, turned their silvery sides to the cool wind as it came from the west, sighing a half-melancholy summer farewell through the lofty pines far above us.

Our boat safely fastened to a sycamore tree near the water's edge, we began our ascent of the mountain—through thickets of hazel and sweet-brier, up through narrow ravines, over ledges of rock, by a sparkling waterfall, through a ragged field on the side of the mountain, on again by a winding path through the forest, with darkened leaves overhead obscuring the sky and the sunlight, up, up, through arbors of laurel and over moss-covered rocks, until we at last gained the summit of the "Round Top" mountain.

And here, high over all surrounding lands, above the tops of the nearest trees, we beheld a scene, such as no pen can describe or pencil paint. Far down beneath our feet was the village, and beyond it away to the northward toward Lebanon, the richly cultivated farms of Lancaster county, dotted with dwellings, with here and there a church spire, or a snug little school-house in the grove, and still farther off to the north, a village, dim in the distance, while the romantic Susquehanna margined in shining silver a picture too vast and beautiful to be comprehended!

To add to the effect, the sky was clear of any cloud, the sun was just setting, while the river, coming down from the westward, mirrored sun-beams in gold and glory as they lingered upon the water. And the cool breeze whispering over the mountain tops, waving to and fro the boughs of ten thousand trees below, as they seemed to bid each other "good night" ere the darkness closed around them, told sweet lessons to our soul, such as we never before enjoyed.

It was calm, still night, around the mountain and along the river shores before we reached our home in the village.

# HONOR THY FATHER AND MOTHER.

One clear, cold, moonlight night in winter time, when the snow was deep in the fields and woods, and when the fire burned briskly on the cottage hearth of many a home among the hills, an old man, weary and lone, tottered tremblingly to the door of a mansion near the road-side, and asked for a night's lodging.

The bright lamp-light gleamed out cheerily from the window-panes, revealing a company of merry dancers within. It was a night of revelry there, and all the world's sorrowing ones without were forgotten in the giddy maze of the dance.

The old man's step was feeble, his voice tremulous with age and cold, and his clothes all tattered and torn by long journeying and wear. He seemed to be an outcast, friendless and forsaken,—a poor pilgrim amid life's storm and trouble, wandering in quest of a home he hoped to find.

See him! that mild, blue eye of his, now moistened by tears as he pleads with the proud man for a single night's rest beneath his roof, how it tells of youth long past!

"Please, sir, I'm very tired and hungry," said the old man, leaning upon his staff, and gazing, oh! so humbly and imploringly into the face of the *world's* hero—the proprietor of a house for pleasure and *fashionable* entertainment, "I've traveled all the day long without a morsel of bread to eat, and now the night has overtaken me, and I must try and get some place to sleep and be refreshed until the morning. I have a dear son somewhere in ——."

"We don't keep public house—neither a house for paupers, old fellow—be off," was the comfortless reception that followed the appeal of the famishing stranger. "If you want lodging, call somewhere else." And with these heartless words the cruel man shut the door, and seated himself to watch the dancers in his comfortable parlor.

And the carousing continued, while the poor, weary wanderer turned into the road and toiled through the deep snow once more!

Would you know whence the old man came, and whither he would go? Listen, and you shall hear.

His only son, Alfred L——, had been a self-willed, disobedient child, and loved the company of idlers better than the sympathy and advices of his father and mother. Many years previous to the winter night of which we speak, Alfred unkindly denied parental authority, and left his early home in England, in a fit of anger and went away to sea. After voyaging for three years from place to place as a sailor, acquiring many of the bad habits of reckless, seafaring life, he at length landed in Philadelphia. Here he found opportunity of indulging in all sorts of wickedness among comrades dissipated and intemperate as himself.

Gambling for drink and for small amounts of money,

(for this class of gamblers seldom have much to risk,) was his pastime, and his only pleasure was in the momentary excitement of a game of cards. Frequent mingling with transgressors, soon made Alfred an expert criminal, so that his whole life had become one of dishonor, shame, and remorse.

From the city Alfred wandered westward, friendless and without money; and even more destitute than all that, he had no disposition to earn a livelihood, and no well-grounded principles by which to establish a fair name in any community. What a want is this!—to want honor. After a tedious and sorrowing journey of several weeks, lodging sometimes in barns or beneath the clefts of rocks on the wayside, pilfering and begging his way from house to house, Alfred at length arrived at a city on the banks of the beautiful Ohio; but the calm river told none of its peace to him. The birds in the forests of Ohio sang their sweetest songs; but they touched not the understanding of the hard-hearted and estranged young man who had forsaken his father's house in lands away beyond the sea. Wherever he lingered—wherever he would go—he was haunted by painful recollections of his crimes. There was no peace for him. He lived merely to hate himself and fear others; judging every one who chanced to cross his path, from the no very flattering promptings of his own wicked nature.

Years passed away, and still Alfred lived a wild rover, unsettled and unhappy. He made a meagre living by cheating honest men, by days' work, or usually by gambling, for his long experience in roguery made him skillful in winning the pocket-possessions of others. And with such unpleasant experiences as these, his years passed away, until middle age found him a bloated sot, the husband of a wife unamiable as himself, and the unloved father of several neglected children.

Some ten years after Alfred L——'s marriage, he invested a few dollars in a lottery ticket—another species of gambling—and drew a prize of several hundred dollars. With this ill-gotten gain he rented a mansion near the city, and kept a kind of public house for dancing and drinking among the middle circles of society.

Only in such unhallowed excitement as this could the miserable man, (for he was, indeed, miserable,) find the means of passing away his time. He had become so dissipated in body and weakened in mind, that his house and himself were subject to the orders of any party of gay frolickers who chose to patronize his bar or revel in his halls.

And that bitter, cold night when an old man called on him for a night's lodging, he was not ashamed to turn the stranger, weary and alone, uncared for away!

Let us go back again to Alfred L——'s early days and his England home. His parents grieved for him, and looked long and anxiously for his return. Years rolled away, and they heard not a single word from their prodigal son. Lost as he was to them, far, far from the hearts that loved him so well, living a life of rioting and disgrace among bachanalians and thieves, yet his fond father and mother loved him still, for Alfred was their own son. They had heard his first words, and enjoyed his innocent sports when he was a child. Oh, how they loved their boy! But their affection was lavished upon an ungrateful, disobedient, wandering prodigal. Yet they waited to welcome him home again. They were

"Her very last words were, I do wonder where my poor Alfred is now—will he ever come home?" Page 189.

faithful and true, while their wayward son forgot his own mother's love and his father's prayers, and preferred to revel with strangers in far distant lands.

By and by the good old mother, after years and years of despondency and grief, died, lamenting her son. Her very last words were, "I do wonder where my poor Alfred is now—will he *ever* come home?"

The father tried to cheer her in her great sorrow; but the dear old man grieved so much himself, that all his looks of comfort came out from eyes wet with weeping over the same grief; and all his words of solace were broken with sobs of sorrow for poor, lost, misguided Alfred.

How stricken and sad was the old father, when his beloved wife was taken from him and laid to rest in the grave! No friends now to join him in sympathy or mingle their tears with his, not one! All gone! And to add to his bereavement, a distant relative rudely took possession of the homestead where Alfred was born, and where so many long years had been passed, and thus the cup of the old man's sorrows was full, and alone he must drink it to the dregs.

By some strange accident about this time, tidings came to him that a man bearing the name of his long lost son, lived somewhere away over the sea; and at once the old father resolved to find him if he could. He accordingly set sail from England, leaving behind him his home now in the keeping of others, his wife now sleeping in the church-yard, and after a short and not unpleasant voyage, arrived on the shores of America, a "stranger in a strange land.'

He traveled about from place to place for nearly a year

in search of his son, but in vain. His money was all gone, his clothes nearly worn out, his strength well nigh spent, when, in his anxious journeyings and almost desponding hopes, he chanced to wander, unknown, to the very door of his son's mansion, where, amid music and dancing, he was denied admission. Strange meeting! How different the reception a loving father would give to a returning prodigal! Yet the father and son knew not they had ever met before.

But poor old pilgrim! spurned of men, yea, by his own child turned out to the piercing cold of a mid-winter midnight, his troubles were nearly ended. He was told to call *somewhere else;* but he needed no more of earth's comforts or consolations. He tottered along a weary mile farther on his way, and then, overcome by cold and hunger, he rested from his toil. He was kindly called from deep distress, such as his trembling body and over-burdened spirit could no longer endure—called home to the "house not made with hands," to the everlasting rest prepared for the *faithful.*

His frozen body was found in the morning, robed in the white snow, and the freed soul, young again, and companioned with his dear wife, was safe from storm and sorrow, for ever with the Lord!

The son, in refusing entertainment to a stranger, had turned not only angels away, but a loving, forgiving, yearning father. When Alfred L—— discovered this terrible truth by papers found in his father's pocket, he felt for once, and thrillingly, the emptiness of all earthly allurements, and is now a sorrowing penitent, but finds no peace. A life like his, sacrificing a father and mother to a death of grief, needs deep, deep repentance. May the erring man yet find forgiveness, and be permitted to meet his dear father and mother in a home where none who anxiously seek rest shall be turned away!

# LAZINESS.

INDOLENCE is one of the fashionable evils of the times. It is a nasty disease, and thousands of unhappy souls die of it. There is a class of persons who make no legitimate use of the faculties God has given them. They are content to drowse away in miserable indifference their talents and their time. The world has no work for them, or, at least, they can not see that it has.

This pernicious influence very easily gets a lodgment in the brains and bones of thoughtless boys; and more especially is this true, when unappreciated and unloved tasks are set before them. Some twisty problem in the mathematics, or some tough and tangled sentence in grammar, discourages the young semi-student: his head becomes dull, his heart heavy, and his whole physical nature limbered into down-right laziness. He forgets the nature and necessity of mental discipline, the utility of vigorous bodily exercise, and the sweet and saving influence of moral culture. He does not succeed, because he fails to realize that the mysteries yet unraveled are all-harmonious in their adjustments. He is allowed to be faithless, wavering, and sprinkle-minded. His first lessons are loose and loveless. He begins to study by the job, and learns to live and move and think *ditto*.

He may, perhaps, be skeptical as to the means employed by his teacher in elucidating difficult theories. He begins to depend on ready-made-to-order thought; stale and printed book-opinions are fresh enough for him. He tires of his Latin and his Lexicon too soon. He means to be a "practical man," and therefore concludes, with rash self-certainty, that *writing* and *declamation* are his proper pursuits, and he practices these alone and by rule. Thus believing and thus acting, (being acted upon, rather,) he naturally becomes passive-minded, submissive to the promptings of a biased judgment. He falls in love with ease, avoids effort, and chooses and uses others' language and others' learning in all his calculations and conduct. He walks in the foot-tracks of others, and if they limped, he will even exert himself to step in their lame path.

What is the result? Stupidity and indifference in every regard. A lazy student, whether of Nature or of Art, will make a trifling, empty-headed man. We do not mean to say there can be no students outside of school or college walls. By no means. He is a true student who investigates, considers, compares, concludes, believes, no matter where his observations. Why! the world is a school-house, and life a lesson. The world is a disciplinary school, designed to fit us for earnest living, after we shall have passed away from its teachings. It is not a resting-place for the weary, neither a playground for sportive idlers. We should not seek repose where only by constant and ardent toil we may profitably live. This is not the place nor the time for slumber. This world is to work in, not to sleep in; and we must prepare to live, and do some good, useful living before we are ready to die. We are not to "spend our years as a tale that is told," in a world where "all our days are numbered."

Let us be diligent, daring, and disciplined, bravely striving for a higher life than this, the reward of patient, self-denying toil. If we are satisfied with the meager rest that the world offers, it is but an evidence that we have no talent to appreciate eternal truths and promises. The sleepiness of sin is only surpassed by the intensity of its sting. Our minds may be lulled to ruin by laziness, but acute remorse shall succeed the slumber.

Teacher, scholar, work! work to day, and always work, until the task is accomplished and your reward well earned.

## TOBACCO TEACHERS.

Yes, teacher, if you use the weed in any form, you thereby teach its use to others, and you are, therefore, a tobacco teacher. Instead of teaching boys temperance, dignity, and independence, integrity, self-control, and cleanliness, you are, it may be unconsciously, though not the less certainly, periling the whole moral, physical, and intellectual being of the pupils committed to your care; for either the juice, the dust, or the smoke of tobacco tends directly to corrupt the heart, to disease the body, and to blunt the brain. Tobacco is a thief. It steals dollars and cents from the pocket, and dignity and sense from the head. What a sad thought that a *teacher* should submit to the slavery of this filthy habit! Rather let any other man be poisoned than he who, by virtue of his profession, has the power to communicate the infection to the bodies and souls of children! "*Example is more powerful than precept.*"

Let the school-room and all its associations be pure. Let tasteful pictures adorn the walls, and bouquets of the sweetest morning flowers smile from every desk! Let the free air of heaven pass through to invigorate, and purify, and bless!—but let the sickening fumes of tobacco smoke, the still nastier stains and stench of the vile leaf, after it has been "rolled as a sweet morsel under the tongue,"—let all such disgusting things as these be confined to lager-beer saloons and the bar-rooms of third-class hotels.

We write this article, because, in our school travels, we have seen teachers who are dearer lovers of the weed than of wisdom; teachers who can enjoy a cigar better than a school-song or a sweet flower; teachers who can chew and spit with more gratification than they can compute a problem in per centage.

And if *teachers* use tobacco, why not *preachers* too? Sure enough! We have in our mind's eye a few of the latter—members of the most holy calling among men—who do indulge in this ugly practice. We have heard ministers preach purity on the Sabbath, and pollute the sidewalks six days out of seven with foul tobacco smoke, mouthed out for decent sinners to inhale! This is right, or else it is wrong. Will the ladies and the children (not disinterested parties) decide? We are glad that instances such as these are rare, but there ought to be none—no, not one.

Reader, think of a scene like this:—Paul, the apostle, you know, was a zealous and consistent Christian minister, and O how eloquently he could preach! Imagine Paul, the powerful, and Timothy, the learned and pious, in a modern pulpit together. Before the solemn services commence, while the audience are all composed to silent meditation, the deep-toned organ filling the sanctuary with rich harmonies the while, Paul says to his Christian brother, "*Timothy, give me a chew of tobacco!*" You smile at the idea. Well, if that would have been in bad keeping with Paul's profession, is it not equally so among modern ministers?

Let us classify. Sabbath-breaking, drunkeness, card-playing, gluttony, prize-fighting, smoking, chewing!— What a brotherhood! Friends, shall we try to teach the young to claim a better kindred, by throwing around them saving influences in the family and in the school?

# VICIOUS LITERATURE.

Parents and teachers are too forgetful of one incumbent duty, viz., the guarding and guiding of the moral natures of the young. Our children, unattended by faithful advisers, are wandering away in forbidden paths, guideless and friendless, treading upon enchanted ground, reveling among dangerous delusions! Call them back; go out after them; save them!

Are we heard? Well, then, again we tell you, teachers, parents, be vigilant; watch your children day and night; look well to their eternal interests, for these are times of peril. Let the influences of the *home*, the *school*, and the *church*, be united, and, as an ark, preserve our dear youth from the destructive deluge of modern infidel literature—the corrupting books and papers that flood our land.

We are in the midst of a plague not less loathsome and insinuating in its encroachments, than the plague of Egyptian locusts; it is the plague of *papers*, poisoned and puffed, and *pressed* upon the people!

> "Papers, books; it makes me sick,
> To think how ye are multiplied;
> Like Egypt's frogs, ye poke up thick,
> Your ugly heads on every side."

We are not an enemy to books and papers, by any manner of means. So far from it, that we could scarcely live away from their company, or without their influences. Indeed, we are most heartily in love with sober, honest books, and plead guilty of flirting occasionally with sensible, well-behaved periodicals. But we do say, that amid such immensely promiscuous mixtures of things trifling and truths thoughtful, there is imminent danger that our eager children may be deceived.

It is *not* "innocent amusement" to peruse those tedious and terrible tales of daggers and death, bombast and blood, feverish imaginations that they are, emanating from burning brains and sin-sick hearts. Away with them! Such readings destroy all taste for history and the sciences. Nature, decorated in her loveliest May, is too homely for the intoxicated fancy of the novel-reader; and life itself becomes a weariness—a disappointment. Religion, so pure, and peaceable, and precious, can not find a welcome or a home in the heart of the passionate novel-reader. Aaron Burr, a man of rare genius and fairest intellectual endowments, reveled in novels and infidel books in his youth, and, as a natural consequence, dwarfed and dwindled down into a traitor's grave!

For the immortal soul's sake, let us awake to a discharge of our duty in this matter. It is high time for us to oppose this latter-day *Satanism*. Call it what you may; mingle as much sugar with the poison as you choose;. apologize for it for ever, if you dare, it is, nevertheless, a deadly dose to all who swallow it. A grain of strychnine is not less fatal from being sweetened with a hundred times its bulk in honey. The mind must have pure, wholesome, nutritious diet, or it will languish and die the second death!

Let us, as Educators and Christians, strive humbly, earnestly, devotedly, prayerfully, to counteract this growing evil. May our hostility to it be mingled with our teachings, henceforth, while life shall last!

## JUNE AND ITS TEACHINGS.

This is the month of robins and roses,—the dearest time of all the year! Now the days are long and warm; the nights are short and still. The young corn is rising in green, laughing rows in the fields; the grass is everywhere carpeted on wide, airy, summer plains—adown in the valleys, upon the hill-sides; the trees are decorated in living green; the birds sing cheerily; the flowers wave lovingly; the waters sparkle laughingly; the clear, blue sky smiles over all, while the gentle airs of summer-time breathe love, and peace, and joy to every soul.

How pleasant it is to take a morning walk in the country, in June! Little boys and girls should rise early, and out and away! A breath of the pure, fresh morning air in June has more virtues than all the medicine ever mixed. The morning is Nature's richest time. The most precious diadems on earth are the cool dew-drops that glisten on the grass, on the leaves, on the flowers, and on the blades of corn! The sweetest perfumes are the fragrant clover-fields,—the honeyed blossoms on the apple-trees,—the early opening flowers of the morning.

While earth is so very fair and joyous, how glorious

must Heaven be! If all these delights are given to poor pilgrims on the way, what great gifts must be in reserve for them at the end of the journey!

Children, did you ever think of this kind promise of the Redeemer? "*I go to prepare a place for you.*" Think of that. The "Friend of friends,"—the same who made his home for awhile with Mary, and Martha, and Lazarus, in their little cottage on the mountain-side, near Bethany,—now ascended on high, and engaged in preparing homes in Heaven for his saints! O, what a happy home he will prepare for you and me, if we love him and obey him! He knows just what kind of a home we need, and its comforts and honors will be far greater than we can now comprehend.

That blessed home, so peaceful and so fair, will be somewhere near the River of Life, in the midst of the City of Gold. Jesus is there now, preparing places for good children, while all around him are multitudes of rejoicing little ones of whom he once said, while on earth, "*Let them come unto me, for of such is the kingdom.*"

Dear children, let this delightful month teach its love and its hope to you. Be happy while you may—while such smiling cheerfulness greets you on every side; but, remember, dear young friends, remember, that neither this merry June nor your glad youthfulness shall remain unchanged. Soon both shall pass away for ever. The lessons of wisdom you learn shall bless you after many days.

## AUTUMNALS.

VERNAL beauties without number,
Summer's charms so fair and gay,
All have gently gone to slumber—
All have quickly passed away,
  Like bright phantoms,
  Or sweet anthems;
All have quickly passed away.

Sad and lonely is the wailing
Of autumnal breezes low,
While the leaves are lightly falling—
Falling silently and slow;
  While the gleaming
  Stars are dreaming,
And the night-winds come and go.

Soon will winter, cold and dreary,
Usher on his dismal train;
Chilling blasts, with wings aweary,
Now proclaim his cruel reign.
  Nature sighing,—
  Beauty dying,—
Now proclaim his cruel reign.

So is Life, though now adorning,
With its hopes, our humble lot,
Transient as the dews of morning—
Like a summer's dream forgot.
    Oh, how fleeting!
    Soon retreating;—
Like a summer's dream forgot.

May we learn that we are mortal,
That from earth we soon remove;
Soon we pass the narrow portal,
Pass from toils to joys above.
    Oh, how cheering!
    How endearing!
Pass from earth to joys above.

# PRIZE FIGHTING.

WHAT is it? Answer: the most doggish business in which anything having the shape of a man can engage. The human body, made in the image of God, reared in a land of schools and Sabbaths, in this enlightened (?) age, to get down below the common respectability of the brutes that perish, is surely humiliating enough! And every vile victory in the *ring*, surrounded by blue-nosed, bloody-eyed, whisky-soaked ruffians, abettors and admirers of deeds that savages are too refined to look upon, only lowers the mock champion deeper in the mire.

Pounding each other in the face—gougings of eyes—bitings of noses—diggings of ribs—all by profession, are so inhuman and disgusting, that we wonder why any dignified person or paper should connive at the prize fight, even so much as to name the *thing* that fought, the place, or time. Some of our literary periodicals come to us with detailed accounts of a recent fight, and with glowing biographical sketches of notorious pugilists. Shame on such *litter*-ature! Why, it would dishonor a decent dog to be complimented on the same page!

Away with such barbarism! It is worse—call it as it deserves—the dirty work of demons incarnate. It is insulting to humanity, to see papers illustrate and encourage this horrible wickedness. We are an advocate of physical culture, and a friend of healthful amusements, and believe they are essential parts of education; but to see a human form so outraged, an immortal soul so forgotten as that of the prize fighter must be, we tremble for the reputation of a community that sanctions the heinous vice by its silence.

Why not speak for the sake of the rising race, and teach them to know that there is a higher, nobler life among men—a life of love to our neighbors, and good will to all?

"Let dogs delight to bark and bite,
For 'tis their nature to—"

But let human beings live for better purpose. True bravery—real moral courage—has a keener grit and keeps better company. It is less presuming, less pompous, *less popular*, but only the more genuine for all that.

# BARRING OUT.

It was a common custom when we were a school-boy in the West, to demand a treat from our teacher the day before Christmas, something in the way of apples—say four or five bushels—some candy, cakes, and oftentimes a little sweet cider, for the sake of variety. If the teacher happened to be a "clever fellow," as the boys would say, and complied becomingly with the request, it would be well for him. If he refused, then the Christmas morning very early would find the door and windows of the school-house firmly fastened against him, with some half-dozen noisy boys *inside*, having a glorious jollification among themselves.

We have known brave sixteen-year olds to rise at two o'clock in the morning and hurry off to the school-house to be on the safe side—the inside—on a cold Christmas. On the outside, when the usual school hour would arrive, might be seen the non-plussed teacher, surrounded by a score or two of half-frozen little urchins, all trying to gain entrance, but held at bay by the young heroes within. And not until a promise written and signed by the teacher that a treat should be forthcoming, would there be the romotest chance for admission.

Well, it was sport for the boys, and not very annoying to the teacher after all, when the apples would be passed around in baskets to the expectant little younglings, all seated in rows to receive their portion of the spoils! The happy, old-fashioned Christmas times in our country schools in Ohio shall never be forgotten. But we hope the time for "barring out" has gone by, as a relic of the past when schools were in their infancy; and that the boys and girls of the present day have more refined notions of the relation of teacher and pupils.

# AN UGLY HABIT.

Youths who whittle, mark or write words, pictures or initials about the school premises, are in a fair way to become hateful. No good person admires such work, or calls it smart. It ought not to be permitted; there is no excuse for it. It is a base ugliness that does it. A successful teacher will effectually suppress such conduct. How? you ask. If you are a teacher, and toil with a will and a zeal for your school's good, you will find a way. You have failed to discharge your whole duty, if you have failed here.

Think of a disfigured, damaged, scored-up schoolhouse! Walls, fences, desks, seats, all bearing the marks of wanton nastiness! A boy who is addicted to this habit, and refuses to break it off at once, will always be a sneak and a nuisance. He will never acquire the frankness and dignity of a man; but will be despised and avoided wherever he goes.

Teachers, strive to get up a universal abhorrence of such a practice among your boys. Be firm in your hostility to it at all times, in all places, and under all circumstances. Do not forget this part of your duty; it calls out your regard for the virtue and nobility of your school, and touches every relation that you sustain to the little community in which you mingle.

If you have the misfortune to be already located in a school-house where the seats, desks, and fixtures have been soiled in this way, tear them down and hide them for ever from the sight. Substitute new, clean, decent furniture instead, and *keep it bright and untarnished*. Do not, for conscience' sake, put in jeopardy the tastes of your pupils, and in no other particular is there greater peril.

## TO THE COMET.

Art thou a prophet—come to tell
    Dread messages of fear?
To warn of sorrow, woe, and ill,
    That hover o'er us here?
Hast thou a voice, and dost thou sound
    To all the list'ning spheres
The wonders of thy mystic round,
    Ne'er told to mortal ears?

Art thou a servant—sent abroad
    By all-creative Might,
To gather from our brilliant orb,
    The wealth of life and light,
To bear away, and shed around,
    In glorious splendor, far
In distant realms—sublime, profound,
    Where new-made planets are?

Far, far beyond the palest star,
    Thine orbit winds its way;
And while thy path extends so far,
    Thou canst not here delay.

## TO THE COMET.

Farther and farther—like a stream
    That flows to ocean's breast,
Thou'lt vanish as a pleasant dream
    In hours of quiet rest.

And wilt thou onward ever run—
    Thy glory still display—
While moon and stars and earth and sun
    Are doomed to pass away?
Whate'er thy mission, thou hast taught
    Sweet lessons to my soul;
Though long thy way—outreaching thought—
    Thou'lt gain thy destined goal.

And as thy radiant wings make bright
    Thy pathway through the skies,
So Faith, and Hope, and Love shall light
    Our way to Paradise!
There shall the soul, with angel-aid,
    Heaven's mysteries explore,
And clouds of doubt that sin hath made,
    Begloom its light no more.

# TEACHERS' CONVENTIONS.

EVERY teacher should be a member of some Educational Association. In every township and village there might be an organization of teachers for the purpose of self-improvement and mutual co-operation in the great work. We would urge upon teachers—and young teachers especially—the importance of working together as a band of brothers and sisters in the education of children.

Isolated effort can not develop human mind. There must be a union of thought, feeling, and power; then the young immortals committed to our care, seeing so much mutual sympathy, so much united toil, so many blended invitations and solicitudes in their behalf, will recognize their teachers as friends indeed, to whom they may turn for guidance and for protection.

Let every teacher resolve to be one of a society having in view the blessed mission of the Great Teacher among men. Gather your professional kinsmen around you, and prepare some plan of union and communion, often, one with another. Call your organization by whatever name you will, Lyceum, Institute, Conference, or Convention, but let it be an *experience* meeting, a place to exchange views, submit plans, correct errors in discipline or instruction, and strengthen the ties of a common brotherhood.

Teacher, trust not to self alone for success. Let God and your brethren influence you. Be firm only for truth's sake. Do not be puffed up in your own notions of human nature's wants and wishes; be social, loving, gentle, long-suffering, and kind. Be child-like without being childish. Be manly without seeking to be like any other man. Be *self* without being *selfish*.

Some teachers are apt to be too high-minded. They think and act at a cold hight far above the heads and hearts of their pupils. Their eyes overlook the glowing beauties of smiling childhood, and rest only on the cold, lone hights of far distances. We must be like little children, confiding, cheerful, earnest-hearted, if we would profitably lead their young souls to know the great world without.

It is down in the valleys where the sweetest flowers grow, the gentlest breezes play, and the purest waters sparkle; and there let us linger and work. The moment a teacher gets up among the mountains in his proud and selfish ambitions, that moment his heart becomes cold and rough as the rocks over which he climbs, and all his school will be frosted over with distrust and doubt. Again, we ask you, teacher, be humble, be honest, be hopeful, willing to join the company and mingle in the employments of the faithful upon earth, and Heaven will bless your toil.

# FISHING

How delightful the soft breezes and the clear waters, that kiss each other in the valleys!

What school-boy but loves to ramble away to the brookside—by the old mill, humming its monotonous music all day long—beyond the meadow, where the tall grass and the water-lilies grow—away to the shade of the ancient sycamore that stands near the bridge and throws its cool shade over a favorite fishing place!

Imagine a boy by the brook-shore, waiting and watching for a bite? As he gazes down into the water, he sees the fishes coming in little companies toward the tempting bait, suspended on an unseen hook, but dangerous to any of the finny tribe that touch or taste, and fatal to every one that swallows it.

See how gracefully they play around the very instrument of death! When the little girls pass over the bridge, their shadows are cast upon the smooth surface of the water, and the fishes dart away in every direction! Afraid of a shadow—and at the same time tampering with the deadly hook suspended right among them! Soon they glide back again, one by one, some of the gayest of them turning on their silver sides, and then circle round the fatal hook once more. A meddlesome minnow gives the bait a slight touch, and then quickly dives out of sight, half frightened at his own escape!

Now a still more venturesome chub goes up, views the tempting morsel from every side, then makes a mouthful of it, gives it a jerk and attempts to swim away,—but, he is caught, and tossed on the grass to die. The other fishes all hide themselves quick as a thought, when they see the unfortunate one snatched from the water; but they as soon forget warning, and the next moment they are ready to run the same risks as before. And so, one after another is caught, until the fisher-boy has a great string of them as the reward for his patience and dexterity.

Little boys and girls may learn a lesson from the silly fishes. Never trifle with temptation; flee from it at once. Never allow yourselves to be deceived by honeyed words or dazzling gifts—there may be a hidden hook there.

## "AWAY UP HIGH!"

Resting, one serene day in summer time, I chanced to loiter awhile in a hill-side church-yard, near a quiet village in the West. Alone, I wandered leisurely around among the little graves, and the long graves, reading and meditating over the different inscriptions on strangers' head-stones. I was far from home, and every name I read was to me an unknown name. No one was there to tell me of the sleeping dead. All was quiet; all was still.

It was a sad and silent spot—the place of burials, yet beautiful. The gentlest airs of summer breathed low, sweet music through the willows there. I was not lonely, for the bright flowers smiled all around, the grass was fresh and green beneath my feet, and the little birds were skipping about and singing right over the graves! While I was standing beside a very little new-made mound, over which the grass had not yet spread its covering of green, a child, with bright, curling ringlets, and large, dark eyes, came running toward me, and as soon as she reached the little grave by my side, she took my hand, and looking at me with a sweet, innocent smile, said:—

"Lillie is not here. She's gone home. Angels took sister Lillie."

"And did you come to tell me that Lillie is not here?" I asked.

"Yes, sir," she said, with a hopeful, earnest look, such as a child-like trust can alone reveal, "Lillie's gone AWAY UP HIGH!" and pointing upward, repeated, thoughtfully, "AWAY UP HIGH!"

O! if we could only look upon death as did that little child! She had not gone to the grave to weep, but to tell a stranger that Lillie was not there, but had gone "away up high."

She thought not of the cold, gloomy grave, but of life and glory beyond. Others, older than she, might weep for the little missing one, but she looked smilingly "away up high!" and her thought was of Lillie in heaven. Dear, sweet, *faithful* child, may you never learn to "fret against the Lord."

I have often thought, since then, that the favorite hymn,

"There is a happy land,
Far, far away,"

may teach the little ones who sing it, that heaven is out of sight; yet the children may well claim

"—— a happy land,"
*Near, near* at hand,

for happiness and peace are ever *near* to the good.

## LITTLE BELIEVERS.

The Christian religion is adapted to the little ones. The young children are embraced in its promises, addressed in its teachings, and may enjoy its comforts.

Religion is life, and peace, and joy. Why should we burden the story of the cross with so many gloomy thoughts of death and the grave? Children love life. It is sweet for them to think of living. Better teach them how to live; for the promises of religion are long life and happiness.

Too many of our juvenile books tell the same sad stories. A good little boy who loves his teacher, and is ever kind and obedient, is always made to die and be buried up in the cold ground, by some over-wise authors and story-tellers in the little books!

We once heard a little boy say, after he had been saddened by the dying pages of a Sunday-school book, "I don't want to be good—all good little boys *die!*"

Let us teach the children that to be good is to *live*. Far wiser to tell them how to live and do good to the living among the living—how to practice the religion we all profess. We must live well, and hope for long life here, for this is the best world we shall find this side of heaven. If we teach the rising race how to rise up into the life and joy of the Christian believer, we are teaching them the upward way to God and eternal peace. If we live right, there will be no trouble about the dying. It will be but dropping the body into sweet repose, and letting the soul go on up home to heaven.

Not long ago we read a story like this: One day a little boy ten years old asked his father if he might join the church. He said he loved the Saviour, and wished he might be among the people of God. "Oh," said the father, "you are too young. Wait till you are older." Now, this boy's father was a shepherd; and it was the little boy's duty to herd the sheep and lambs; that is, to gather them in the folds at night, so that the wolves and wild beasts might not harm them. One night his father said to him, as usual, "My son, have you gathered them all in?" "I believe so." "All?—are you quite sure?" "Oh, I have got them all in except that little lamb that is so young and weak; I thought I would leave him out now, and bring him in when he grew older, and got a little stronger!" The reproof went to the father's heart. Before long that little boy joined the church.

This little story was related, a short time ago, in a Sabbath-school meeting, and it moved one little girl, who felt that she loved the Saviour, but was too young to join the church. The last we heard of her was that she had come out and professed the name of Christ before the world.

## MY SISTER'S GRAVE.

BENEATH yon lone willow
   My dear sister lies,
There soft is her pillow,
   And closed are her eyes.
'Tis there she reposes,
   Where sweets ever new—
Bright violets and roses
   Are washed with the dew.

I kneel where she slumbers
   And silently pray,
When in calm, flute-like murmurs,
   A voice seems to say:
"O! why should ye sorrow?
   And why should ye sigh?
'Twill be as to-morrow,
   When here all must lie."

Those low, plaintive vespers
   That float o'er her tomb,
Are the soul's gentle whispers
   That breathe of its bloom
In spheres of pure brightness,
   In regions divine,

## MY SISTER'S GRAVE.

Where saints clad in whiteness,
   And cherubim shine.

A harp has been given
   To sister above,—
She tunes it in heaven
   To anthems of love;
While echoes of gladness
   Resound through the sky,
That she, freed from sadness,
   Now triumphs on high!

# THE LOVE OF CHRIST.

*Jesus Christ, the same yesterday, and to-day, and for ever.*—HEB. XIII. 8.

WHAT a declaration is this! How encouraging! While we are tossed to and fro on the stormy sea of earth-life—our frail bark well nigh overcome by the swelling waves of sin, our souls weary with the tedious pilgrim voyage—there is a clear, unwavering light, gleaming from the "shining shore," far out over the waters between us and our haven of rest. That beacon light is this comforting assurance: "Jesus Christ, the same yesterday, and to-day, and for ever."

Christ's person, his power, his love, his grace, and his glory, are unchangeable. The *yesterday* of Jesus is all the gone-by of eternity, and infinite past. His *to-day* is the present. His *for ever* the unending future. He is "from everlasting to everlasting the same."

His love to sinners had no beginning; he loved us before the foundation of the world. Neither can such love have an end. Earthly loves soon grow cold and die; but Jesus' love is Divine and can not cease. It can not change. How consoling the thought that this same blessed Lord deigns to love us, and has called us with a holy calling! We may approach him, all-sinful as we are, and commit our souls, troubled and sin-sick, to his gracious, pitying love; for his own precious blood has redeemed us. Oh, this boundless ocean of the Saviour's love! Who can comprehend it?

We cherish our earthly friends. We can tell our sorrows to those who are near and dear to us here. We often mingle our tears in social soul-communings with our beloved companions, around whom twine our fondest affections. And these minglings of sorrows, these free-flowings of tears, these unreserved expressions of our desires and our fears, our doubts and our griefs, afford us relief and make life less weary to be borne.

But the best of earthly friends may forsake, or change, or die. No other trust, no other hope is steadfast, save in Jesus, "the same yesterday, and to-day, and for ever." His grace will be sufficient for us in every trial and in every trouble. To be a loved one of Jesus is to be safe. His arms alone will bear us safely over to the other shore. Our poor human love can ascend in fervent prayer-breathings, and unite with Jesus' love Divine —Jesus, once on earth, a "man of sorrows and acquainted with grief;" surely, he knows our infirmities, and will hear the suppliant when he cries! Jesus, the crucified and risen Saviour; surely, he will forgive the sins of the poor penitent who asks in faith, believing! Jesus, the ascended Lord of glory; surely, he will receive to himself, in his heavenly kingdom, all who trust his promises, and have been washed in his own blood! Jesus—"the same yesterday, and to-day, and for ever."

Oh, his willingness to save! Hear him: "Come unto me all ye that labor and are heavy laden, and I will give you rest." Mark his ability to save: "If ye shall ask any thing in my name, I will do it." And then think of his waiting to save. "Behold, I stand at the door and knock." Yes, blessed be his name! His willingness, his ability, his anxiety to save are always the same, the same.

Who, who will come, and rest, and rejoice for ever in the boundless, undying love of Jesus? Let your resolution and your song be—

> "Just as I am, without one plea,
> But that thy blood was shed for me,
> And that thou bidst me come to thee,
> O Lamb of God, I come.
>
> "Just as I am, thy love unknown
> Has broken every barrier down;
> Now to be thine, yea thine alone,
> O Lamb of God, I come."

## SUMMER.

THESE sultry August days, oh, how wearily they do linger! There is scarcely a breeze astir among the forest leaves to tell that *real* summer is not a *picture*—all Nature around is so quiet and still!

The shades beneath the old beech-trees, and the peaceful brook, half hidden by the weeds and grass, seemed never so refreshing as to-day. How gratefully the patient cows drink from the cooling and thrice-welcome water!

But soon these hot summer days will have gone by, and we shall remember them as among the things of the "Long Ago."

These leaves so fair and green to-day will soon wither and fall, and mix with clay again. And so with us, dear reader. To-day we are hopeful and well—very soon we sicken and die; and these bodies of ours moulder into their native dust. But the soul shall live for ever. That is like God. Its home is heaven; and when we get there, we shall find purer waters, and sweeter rest, than earth can afford. And no change shall take our joys away, or part us from the friends we love. Oh, to be there!

## MEMORY OF EMMA*—A PUPIL.

THE messenger came in the time of roses, when all our joys were full. He came, and our sunshine faded into night; our merry school songs languished into tearful lamentations for the dead! EMMA, our dearest playmate—EMMA, who ever came, and lingered, and went away, smiling, always smiling, for she knew nothing but love, was invited to an angel-party in the skies, and she came not back again. She was loved here, but loved more in heaven. And so Jesus called her to his own home, to sing and play with his little angels there! While our heads are bowed in sorrow at our loss, and while our hearts go mourning all the day long, our darling has already

> "A crown upon her forehead—
> A harp within her hand."

But the grave!
It is hard to believe it, that we shall see her no more—no more listen to the melody of her song. EMMA was a pleasant, a lovely child—the beloved one of her teach-

---

\* EMMA, daughter of J. M. and Nancy Douglass, died, June 18 1858, aged eleven years.

ers and schoolmates all. But she is dead. Her little heart is not beating now. She is pale and still. Yet we remember her form and her features. We mourn because our EMMA is not here. She sleeps in the church-yard with others who have departed. She was never in so cold and hard a bed, but she feels it not. She will never feel pain or grief any more—her suffering time is over.

Her bed is dark, and damp, and chill; but there is no fear, nor gloom, nor weeping there—O, no! all is sweet peace, and she rests. Let her sleep on and take her rest. Plant evergreens and roses over her grave, and let her sleep on in quietness among the foliage and the flowers. Her spirit is with God who gave it. Yes, EMMA loved flowers. I remember now,—she used to bring amaranths, daisies, and white lilies, and lay them before me on my desk at school. Now the angels have come and taken *her*—an *immortal* flower—to heaven's fair bowers away. Sweet thought! Our darling child now in the glad company of angels, and singing with angel-bands! Why are we sad? Oh, we miss her so! Alas! we miss her; but she is not lost—only "gone before."

Hers was a kind, confiding disposition. She loved everybody, and everybody loved her. How often has she taken my hand in both of hers, and, with smiles of affection, invited me to her village home! That invitation is still extended. She now invites me, and all of us, to her new and eternal home in the Celestial City. Sisters, and dear little brothers, father and mother, and schoolmates, dry up your tears. Weep no more. We indeed have a "*treasure* in heaven!" May "our hearts be there also!" We hope to meet her in glory.

## IN MEMORY OF EMMA—A PUPIL.

"Heaven's dews drop mutely on the hill;
The cloud above it resteth still,
　　Though on its slope men toil and weep,
More softly than the dew is shed,
Or cloud is floated overhead,
　　'HE GIVETH HIS BELOVED SLEEP!'"

# HONEST WILLIE.

One beautiful morning in spring, as little Willie S―― was hurrying along through the woods to school, he found a pocket-book in his path, close beside the brook. When he first observed it, he was running along, thinking of his lessons at school, and wishing to be there among the class-mates he loved so well. He was happy as the birds that sang and skipped about among the branches over his head.

Willie was poor, and his mother was a widow. His first thought, on picking up the pocket-book, was one of joy that he would find it full of money. He opened it and found great rolls of bank notes and several pieces of gold. He thought of his poor mother; then of new clothes, and books, and a thousand other things that money buys, and said to himself, "Now we shall be rich!" But all this while, there was a "still small voice"—*it seemed like his own dear mother's*—telling him to "Beware." The tender young leaves whispered it in his ear, and the birds began to warble it in the trees, "Beware—honesty is the best policy!" Willie then thought of his mother's counsels and of her prayers, then of his own happy home, humble as it was, and resolved to keep the treasure only until he could find the owner for it.

He put the pocket-book safely in his little satchel, hastened homeward again, and told his mother all about it, not forgetting to tell her how he had been tempted. She embraced her beloved boy with tears, and said, in the same tender tones that Willie thought he heard when he was alone with the tempter, "You have brought me a far richer gem than gold, my son, *an honest heart.* Cherish the principles of truth and honesty as the most precious treasures of your life. I am proud of you, Willie."

In a few minutes, Willie was off again to school, happier and richer than ever gold has made any one feel. It was not long until the owner of the lost pocket-book heard that Willie S—— had found it; and he felt no more uneasiness, for he knew Willie was an honest boy and would return it. And so he did. *Such* a boy could not act dishonestly, for his mother's constant prayers had brought guardian angels down to be company for Willie every day.

Willie was offered a handsome reward, but very manfully declined it, saying that his mother's love, and God's smiles, and his sweet angel company, were the best rewards he could desire.

Need I tell you, young reader, that this little boy is now one of the greatest of living men? Some time I may tell you his name; you have heard it often.

## HOW DO YOU LEARN?

CHILDREN, the above question is for you to answer. We may aid you in answering it by means of the following illustration:

Passing along by a very pretty farm-house in one of the western counties of Ohio, one summer day, we observed a man pouring water from a bucket into the top of an old pump that stood in the yard.

We did not at first understand why the man should pour water *into* the pump; we had always supposed that water was drawn *from* pumps when it was wanted. If he had more water than he could use, the dry, thirsty ground would gladly receive it all! Why did he pour it back through the pump into the well again?

We watched the man for a long time. He would first pour a bucket of water into the pump-stock, then seize the pump-handle and work as though he wished to draw all the water out again. But very little water could he get. Even part of what he had poured in was wasted. He kept on, however, pouring in water, bucket-full after bucket-full, and violently working the pump-handle, until at last, the pure, fresh water from the deep well came pouring from the spout in a copious stream! Then he filled his bucket with the cold water from the bottom of the well, and was thus paid for all his trouble.

That old, crazy pump is like a great many children in school! you, and you, and you! I will tell you why. You want the teacher to *pour* knowledge into your heads, instead of searching for it, yourselves. Then when you come up to recite, you tell back only what the teacher has told you before; and some of that is wasted or forgotten. You depend upon what *others* know, and care nothing about reaching outward for new, fresh truths. This is wrong, and it is exceedingly unpleasant. If you would excel, and be wise and happy always, you must draw thoughts from the deep, pure fountains of the soul, and not be content with skimmings, or borrowed thoughts. The teacher may present you with a few thoughts, but receive them as suggestive, and respond to them as such. The true teacher anticipates your help. Meet him half-way. Show him that you feel an interest in your studies. Your progress is dependent, not on what the teacher does for you, but what you do yourselves. Act for yourselves, candidly, perseveringly, independently. *Your education depends on your own exertions.*

# HOW DO YOU TEACH?

Teacher, do you think of the nature and tendency of your daily instructions in the school-room? Are you filling the minds of your pupils with thoughts as well as words? Do you encourage them to think for themselves? Do you teach them self-government?

These subjects should engage a portion of your thoughts every day—every hour—every moment. When the labors of the school-day are closed, the children all gone to their homes, and the quiet evening finds you wending your way homeward to your needed rest, then reflect for a few moments upon the impressions that have been made, the principles inculcated, and the discipline enjoined, during the day that has just passed.

Think of the value of the soul that you are educating, and resolve to bestow your most solicitous attention to every duty devolving upon you as a teacher. See that you work not with unskillful hands. Firmly oppose every influence calculated to interfere with the welfare of your work. Such a course imparts confidence to the entire school.

Be willing to receive suggestions and advice from persons whose age, experience, and position, entitle them to respect, and enable them to speak understandingly, remembering that your whole business is to aid in developing and disciplining mind for the enjoyment of an eternal future, by imparting thoughts and principles.

Tasking is not teaching. Demand thought, mental action, from your pupils—not mere words and phrases, that have become stale and meaningless by repetition. Originality of thought is the great want among teachers, as well as pupils. Banish all parrot-work; our children can never become wise by rote—never!

Method is directly opposed to routine task-work. One is harmonious and vivifying—the other, monotonous and stupid. We have an abundance of *machines* already, without converting our children into such, by our ignorance or neglect. Better teach them to teach themselves, reason for themselves, and invent for themselves.

In conducting recitations, it is well to avoid all such questions as may be answered by *yes* or *no*. Ask questions in an easy, familiar manner, but frame them so as to draw out a concise, intelligent answer. The very first duty of the young teacher is to learn how to ask questions.

# COURAGE, TEACHER!

Your work is arduous, we know; but be not discouraged. Though clouds may, at times, overshadow your pathway, press forward—there is light ahead! Though you may not gain the approbation of every one; though you may not win sympathy from the cold-hearted, nor gain the esteem of the indifferent, yet yours is a glorious toil! Faithful laborer, let your heart be glad, for you shall receive an enduring reward of love and joy, if you faint not!

Those young, bounding hearts that beat so warm for you, are yours to guard and cheer. What precious jewels are entrusted to your care! You are surrounded by ardent affection; her sweet whispers are ever in your ear; her silent, though confident prayer-breathings oftentimes ascend to the throne of the All-Father in quest of blessings for you! Your charge is precious, immortal. Only think of it—training *minds* for future weal or woe!

One of the Roman Kings, in pursuing some of his military schemes, once had occasion to cross the Adriatic Sea. Finding no other way, he hired a humble boatman to row him across. The King's errand was important, and must be accomplished. While in the midst of the sea, a violent storm arose; the poor boatman was greatly alarmed and relaxed his efforts in dismay. He was appalled by the threatenings that surrounded his frail bark; his heart was fainting within him, when the future Emperor of Rome thus spoke: "*Courage, my man! you carry Cæsar and his fortunes!*" This address, made in the strength of hope and heroism, aroused the boatman to renewed effort; the storm was successfully outridden, and the gallant King safely landed upon the desired shore.

Teacher, you carry more than "Cæsar or his fortunes." Be vigilant, prayerful. Be not "weary in well doing." Strive manfully, heroically against the obstacles that surround you. Mount upward with faith and hope above the clouds that obscure the sun and the glory, and claim Divine aid in so noble a conquest; and be "not faithless but believing."

And if your zeal and devotion are manifested in persevering effort, your love for the labor shall be at once and for ever your success, your delight, and your reward.

## CONTRASTED SIMILES.

*"The Lord is good."*—NAHUM I. 7.

### I.

THE vernal light, adorning
   Each day with beams renewed,
Seems telling us at MORNING,
   "The Lord is ever good."

The gentle luke-like VESPERS
   That murmur through the wood,
In quiet breathings, whisper,
   "The Lord is ever good."

### II.

The fragrant SPRING, displaying
   Her beauteous flowerhood
Along the vales, is saying,
   "The Lord is ever good."

As AUTUMN strews before us
   Her plenteous stores of food;
Let all respond in chorus,
   "The Lord is ever good."

### III.

Those sunny days of PLEASURE,
   When cares do not intrude,
Speak sweetly this glad measure,
   "The Lord is ever good."

When clouds of sorrow near us
   In hours of SOLITUDE,
Still, still do these words cheer us,
   "The Lord is ever good."

### IV.

The FOUNTAIN, failing never,
   That sparkles in the wood,
With rippling voice says, "Ever—
   'The Lord is ever good.'"

That terror-striking wonder,
   Niagara's mighty FLOOD,
Repeats in tones of thunder,
   "The Lord—the Lord is good."

### V.

A CHILD'S light, merry laughter
   Proclaims in cheerful mood,
As echo answers after,
   "The Lord is good—is good."

The MAN whose frame is riven,
   By age and servitude,
May raise his eyes to heaven,
   And say, "The Lord is good."

## 'TIS SWEET TO REMEMBER.

It is sweet to remember the bouquets our pupils used to put on our desk in the village school-room in the Mays and Junes of years gone by. It cheered our heart to receive such tender tokens of affection from the hands of the dear children with whom we daily mingled in study and in song. The fragrance of flowers wields a sweet influence in the school.

When the flower-time of the year comes, let every little hand be cunning to cull the rarest bouquet for the teacher. Cover him all over with flowers, if you choose, and love him with all your heart. Fill the whole school with flowers, and music, and smiles, and your time will then pass pleasantly and profitably away.

As you trip along to the country school, in the early summer mornings, you will find daisies, and violets, and roses on the way-side; select the very fairest of them all for your teacher. Flowers have their uses.

"Then wherefore, wherefore were they made,
All dyed in rainbow light?

All fashioned with supremest grace,
　　Up-springing day and night!
To comfort man—to whisper hope,
　　Whene'er his face is dim,
For whoso careth for the flowers,
　　Will much more care for him."

## QUIT THAT.

Quit what? Quit telling your innocent, confiding, trembling children about ghosts and hobgoblins. You are throwing a sorrow upon young hearts that will cling there through life. How many mothers there are who quiet their children by saying, "The bug-a-boos will come and take you off!"—"Come, old nigger, come and —well, will you *hush*, then, this minute?"

The poor child believes all its own mother says, and why shouldn't it? It ought to believe. That is its filial duty. The sobbing, fluttering heart is quieted, but not composed. Those tearful eyes close in a sleep of terror; a weary, broken rest follows; the child dreams—but oh! who can tell the sadness of a child while it dreams in a sleep frightened upon it by alarms of all that is terrible and repulsive?

Such inhuman treatment endangers the mind—the intellect. Mothers, beware! And see that no nurse or servant, or older brother or sister, drive arrows of grief to the very soul of your child. A sorrow early planted and watered by tears will bring forth a harvest of bitterness and despair.

How common a habit is this to teach children to fear unseen dangers at nightfall! The peaceful night; so full of sweetness, the night that brings the honeyed drops of dew to bless the flowers and refresh the leaves, and the night that brings rest to the weary, this dearest time of all, is to be made terrible to children. What wickedness! Why, it is blasphemy to make the little ones believe that God forgets them, and sends tormentors to trouble them in the silent watches of the night.

Parents, think of this. See that your children hear no ghostly lessons. See that they are taught to love the ever present Saviour, and to honor his blessed name.

How heavenly the teachings of that familiar hymn, when breathed from a true mother's soul over a sleeping child :—

> "Hush, my babe, lie still and slumber,
> Holy angels guard thy bed!"

## CHRISTMAS TIME.

CHRISTMAS, dear old Christmas, is here. How many kind wishes—how much good cheer it brings! Bright, smiling faces—glad hearts, fond remembrances! Sweet Christmas—dear Christmas, with its fun and frolic for the children, and its genial gifts for all! For all? Alas! for many Christmas brings naught but cold and sorrow. Pity those poor little bare-footed ones. They have been overlooked, forgotten. Why not give *them* nice presents, and hear their artless giggles and shouts as they think of the gifts that let light and gladness into their young hearts?

A gift to the poor and unexpectant! How doubly precious it must be! The poor "we always have with us;" let us make them happy, if we can. They are our kindred. Their hearts are weary and sad. Let us comfort them.

Glad day this! The birth-day of the PRINCE OF PEACE.

> "Christ was born on Christmas-day.
> Wreathe the holly, twine the bay."

What a gift to the fallen world! A Saviour—a King. But we are so forgetful of the mission of this advent.

Our crimes brought him from heaven, and crucified him. Now let the sunshine of a sincere, devoted love illuminate our minds, and earnest, undying confidence strengthen us!

How the dear Christmas time awakens the affections! Let us remember in charity those of whom Christ said, "Inasmuch as ye did it unto the least of these, ye did it unto me." Let us lend a helping hand to the weary poor, in this cold winter time. Let us keep our hearts warm towards those less favored and less happy than we.

## CALLED FROM THE FOREST.

MILFORD MARTIN, and his son James, an industrious lad of twelve, went to the woods one sunshiny morning, in autumn, to cut fire-wood for the approaching winter days. Mr. Martin was a kind, Christian man, and was never known to do a wrong act to a neighbor; and everybody loved him for his gentle good nature, and his many deeds and words of kindness.

He owned a little farm, and kept it in the very best state of culture; every field was comely and productive, every fence neat and straight, every shade tree vigorous and thrifty. His dwelling house was a neat and pretty white frame, and stood close by the orchard, where the big apples hung in ripened beauty on the fruitful trees, or lay in piles here and there upon the grass, where Mr. Martin and James had gathered them the day before they went to cut wood.

Mrs. Martin was a dear woman, and seemed the very happiest one in all the family circle, and was busy that day in preparing something nice for James and his father to eat after the hard day's work. Mary and Lizzie, both younger than James, were trying to be useful about the kitchen, helping their mother to pare the apples for the pies, or fetching in chips to make a hot fire under the supper-kettle.

Mr. Martin had taken especial care to teach his children the great truths of the Bible, and often and often would he tell them about the uncertainty of this life, and how wrong it was to live only for the present. He talked much of a happier home, and of a longer life, in heaven.

As they were walking to the woods that morning, Mr. Martin said, "James, my boy, these autumn days are mild and lovely, but it makes me think of the 'passing away' of life, to see these leaves whirling and rustling to the ground. Did you ever think of the Tree of Life, whose leaves never wither nor fall? Here we need lessons like these to teach us of our mortality. Our time here is short. Remember the teachings of the falling leaves."

"Yes, father, but the glad spring-time brings us new leaves and fresh flowers, and that brightness makes up for these gloomy days. I wish the spring would come again."

"True, and we are just like the leaves; these bodies of ours, sooner or later, we can not know the time, will fall to the ground and moulder away into dust again. But the soul shall blossom anew and for ever in the paradise of God, if we love Him and one another here upon the earth."

James said nothing more, for he thought his father was more solemn than he ever appeared before. Indeed, Mr. Martin's voice was unusually sad, he knew not why himself.

They remained all day in the woods, and toward evening James wandered a little distance away in the forest in search of nuts, and while he was looking about among the brown leaves on the ground and gathering chestnuts for his little sisters at home, he heard the falling of a tree in the direction of his father—then a sudden scream—it was his father's voice calling him, and, oh, how terrible it seemed! Could it be possible that the tree had fallen on his own dear father? In a few minutes he was at the spot, and there lay Mr. Martin crushed and bleeding, beneath a ponderous tree which had fallen upon him!

James was terror-stricken, and in his agony of grief he ran toward home, crying loudly for help. The faithful dog which had followed them to the woods was first at his dying master's side; and when he saw the mangled body, howled in such sad tones that the forests even echoed back the sorrow. But before help came, the spirit of the good man had been released from its clay, and was with the angels! So sudden, so appalling was this stroke upon the family, that it was feared Mrs. Martin would die of grief for her husband. But the heart of woman is often called to bear burdens that would seem too heavy and sad to be endured.

It was a fearful visitation, but the patient Christian family kissed the rod that scourged them so keenly; for they knew there would be a meeting time by-and-by. Fatherless, but not forsaken were those sobbing children, as they stood around the grave of their beloved father. And that widow's tears were not from eyes no more to be comforted by the glimpse of her companion, for she had eyes of faith that beheld him happy and at home. And the afflicted family will not fear the messenger when he shall come to summon others to the father's side. Truly, "we know not what a day may bring forth."

# GOING THROUGH THE WORLD.

There are many ways of going through the world. The school is a world in miniature. As boys go through the school, so will they pass through the world. It is the teacher's duty to guard and guide the children; to cultivate in them habits of industry and self-reliance; and to counteract the ever-present and dangerous influences that surround the young. And these helps must be prominent in the school. Character can not be moulded in a book. There are outside teachings, holier and more enduring, above books, beyond books, better than books. The young man must be taught how to go through the world.

Commonly, men do not recognize a future life, if we are to judge from what we see manifested in their words and acts. The present, with its cares, its perplexities, its doubts, and its tears, is the sole object for which many are wearing their lives away. The present is to them all of existence. The world is all they know, and in it, and for it, and through it, what a toil is theirs! We mention a few ways of going through the world.

A large number *sleep* through. Indifference and sloth have paralyzed their energies; and but for a mere *being*, they are content to live. They take the journey in a sleeping-car in broad daylight; they put forth no effort, feel no anxiety, know no purpose, show no zeal. The world is not benefited by such lives; such lives receive no benefit from the world.

Others *jam* their way through the world. A constant restlessness disturbs their minds and mars their enjoyment. They are not content to "labor and wait," but are always fretting, and pushing, and unnecessarily driving their work. Such characters sacrifice system and order for the sake of confusion and wreck. The world is disturbed by such men; such men are disturbed by the world.

Some *fight* their way. Let any obstacle be presented to impede their progress, or any unforeseen hindrance beset them, and their tempers at once become ruffled and unmanageable, and they are ready to quarrel with all they meet. Rage takes the place of reason, and danger is incurred and wounds received without just cause. Anger becomes the result of difficulty, and overthrow the result of anger. Such men disgrace the world; the world hates such heedless fools.

Not a few individuals *sponge* their way through the world. They live upon the honest earnings of others. Of all sorts of meanness, the *sponge* is the very meanest. He is anybody's—everybody's—nobody's friend. He grows fat on other people's gravy. He pretends to help and counsel only that he may hinder and suck. As long as he is allowed to be a calf he will find a teat. He eats other people's bread, wears other people's clothes, and reads other people's newspapers. He has nothing of his own but his meanness, and he is welcome to that.

The world would be better without such a man; such a man had better be out of the world.

Now and then we find a *sneak*, dodging and disguising his way through the world. You never catch his eye. His look is downcast and ashamed. He knows no firmness, no honor, no integrity, no candor. These manly qualities are utter strangers to him. He tattles, surmises, guesses, tells out-right falsehoods, and then dodges and ducks like a silly goose when no one is threatening or pursuing! He is too simple to devise, and too cowardly to perform a noble act. He would "steal acorns from a blind hog," if we may borrow a phrase to suit the person. He would tremble at an enraged pismire! Such a man will sneak through life abhorred; and sneak out of the world unhonored and unlamented.

Quite a number of half-awakened ignoramuses are found *crawling* through the world. They mean nothing good and do nothing very bad; but they are so inexcusably superstitious and abominably lazy that life is a burden to them. They have a rank growth of flesh and bone, but a poor, puny intellect. They live only to eat, and sleep, and breathe; and thus their existence is rather a beastly than an intellectual one. All the reforms and inventions of the age are mysteries to them—unstudied, wonderful mysteries. Schools and sermons are but idle speculations to their comprehension, and newspapers they use only to light cigars! The world is gloomy and stupid with such burdens as these to bear. Such men help to curse the world; and the world is but little better than a curse to such men.

Another class *lie* their way through the world. They

*tongue* for money—*tongue* for bread—*tongue* for reputation. If a falsehood will fetch a farthing, out it goes after it. No matter how well the truth may suit, it is seldom used by them. They not only falsify by their words, but by their actions also. They deceive by their looks, their manners; even their shapes are libels on manhood. Such men live to cheat the world; the world is too easily cheated by such men.

A few grandmotherly dyspeptics *grieve* through the world. Every breath they breathe is a sigh—every thought a sad one. Life's purest, most ennobling joys are pronounced "vanity" by their sepulchral voices; melancholy and grievous are their poor, forsaken hearts all the while. They are never known to smile. Their pale faces—so long and solemn—remind one of tombstones and ghosts. They hate song, frown upon the sports of childhood, and mourn for the happy-hearted. Nothing pleases them, no matter how proper and good. They are a sickly set of scolds, and sour as crab-apples. They cling to the world with the utmost tenacity, but the world doesn't need them.

A great many persons *laugh* through the world. They are tickled because they have been fortunate enough to be born,—pleased with the most trifling and transient joys of earth. Nothing solemnizes them—nothing alarms them. They are the chaff of society, and are puffed hither and thither by the empty air. They laugh alike at fortune and calamity. They think of nothing but the present. You can coax nothing earnest out of them, but a hearty laugh. They enjoy themselves, and do not aim to mar the peace of others, but their very existence seems to be a farce. Merriment plays the mischief with them ultimately. Such persons trifle away their lives; the world is none the less sincere without them.

A very few *climb* through the world. Most of our readers have read the story of ambitious William, who climbed and carved his name high over all other names on the flinty rocks at the Natural Bridge in Virginia. Only let such an ambition as his sparkle from every eye, and bound from every heart, and ours would be a lively world. After he had engraved his name, he saw to what a giddy hight he had attained, and his only escape was to climb again higher and higher, cutting niches in the hard rock for his feet and fingers, until at last, he was met by kind hands from above, and saved from a terrible death.

And so do all earnest souls triumph at last! There are angel hands to reach down and lead the faithful climber in life's upward way. If a young man would come off victor in the world's strife, and attain to eminent usefulness, he must be ambitious, persevering, prayerful. Then will kind influences from above meet and greet him as he climbs. Young man, choose your way.

# CONTENTMENT.

One cold winter's night not long ago, a poor beggar woman, with her shivering, starving little daughter about four years old, was wandering along one of the most dismal streets of New York City. They had no home, no friends, no supper, no bed! They were very weary and sad. At length, they entered a miserable alley in an unfrequented part of the great city, and came to an old out-house, where the weary, famishing mother found a broken cellar-door on the ground, which she leaned up beside a dirty wall, and under this poor shelter she crawled with her suffering child tightly folded in her arms, for a single night's lodging. The little girl hugged close up to her mother's bosom, and soon began to get warm and sleepy there. The poor child felt so grateful even for that cheerless bed, that she looked up in her mother's face and said, with child-like earnestness, "Mother, what do *poor* folks do who have no cellar-doors in cold winter nights?" There is a definition to the word *Contentment*.

# CHIROGRAPHY.

GOOD penmanship does not consist in spread-eagle flourishes and five-story capitals! True, there should be a freeness of movement in the hand and arm evidenced by the pen-tracings, but never any extravagances. We like a plain, round hand-writing. That is the best piece of chirography which is most easily read. Affected penmanship, like mock polish of any sort, is devoid of grace and beauty.

We hear of some great men who are not good penmen, but their faulty penmanship does not make them great. We know of some half-hatched lawyers, and aspiring young men of other vocations, who claim to be great and distinguished in proportion to the awkwardness and unintelligibleness of their scribbling-ship. And if such were the gauge of guessing at greatness, how *incomprehensibly* great some men would be!

A good story is told of the wretched writing of a certain celebrated railroad manager in Michigan. He had written a letter to a man on the Central route, notifying him that he must remove a barn that in some way incommoded the road, under the penalty of prosecution. The threatened man was unable to read any part of the letter but the signature; but he took it to be a *free pass* over the road, and used it for a couple of years as such, none of the conductors being able to dispute his interpretation of the document!

# THE TEACHER'S POSITION.

"Can't please everybody." No, you can not, nor should not. "Everybody" is a mixed compound of every sentiment—good, bad—intelligent, stupid,—and, consequently, couldn't be pleased with the true teacher's consistency, or with the quack teacher's pliability.

The teacher should study, carefully, his position, understand all its bearings, and guide his actions by the Golden Rule of conduct; and even then, he must expect to incur displeasure. There are habitual growlers, prejudiced critics, and constitutional ignoramuses in the compound, "Everybody," and you may *indirectly* hear from them occasionally! Such individuals never visit your school. They surmise, quiz, guess, presume, pervert, imagine, and manufacture, until their minds are worked into a state of hectic uneasiness. A visit to the school-room might relieve their troubled minds; but, no, indeed! They are resolute *talkers*, yet imbecile *doers* of magnanimous deeds!

Unless the teacher have a heart to forgive, a will to work, a confidence to trust, and a nerve to maintain, surrounded by such influences, he may, at times, become discouraged and go astray.

But there is a brighter side to this picture. By a course of correct instruction in school, upright, moral action without, and an earnest confidence in God for guidance, entire success and general satisfaction will follow the teacher's labors. The young, with their uncorrupted love, are on his side, and here is his strongest hope. The intelligent, warm-hearted, progressive portion of community is on his side, ready to suggest, advise, cheer, and comfort in time of trouble, and here is his trust. God, into whose ear he breathes his desires and feelings, is on his side, and here is his STRENGTH.

The devoted teacher is sufficiently fortified to withstand the confused attacks of the uneducated and presuming. They may attempt, but can not succeed, either in harassing his aims, overturning his work, or distressing his thoughts. Be sure that your theory is right, your heart faithful, then be firm in the defence of the truth. Never mind the breezes!

## A NIGHT OF GLOOM.

"Into the Silent Land!
Ah! who shall lead us thither?
Clouds in the evening sky more darkly gather,
And shattered wrecks lie thicker on the strand,
Who leads us with a gentle hand
Thither, O thither,
Into the Silent Land?

"Into the Silent Land!
To you, ye boundless regions
Of all perfection! Tender morning visions
Of beauteous souls! The Future's pledge and band!
Who in Life's battle firm doth stand,
Shall bear Hope's tender blossoms
Into the Silent Land!"—*From the German of Salis.*

THE cold winter of 185– lingered until late in March, making many of the humble homes of the world's poor comfortless by his tedious snows and biting winds; for the winter stores of fuel and provisions among the farmers in the vicinity of the Old Log School House, were well nigh exhausted. It was one of the dreariest, bitterest nights of all that long winter—a night when the winds wildly chased each other over the hills, leveling the trees in the forests, and scattering the fences over the bare fields, while the full moon, like an immense ball of silver tossed out among the golden stars, rolled along her high-way of sky, revealing herself at quick intervals through the partings of the clouds—when Mrs. B—— arose from her chair by the feeble fire, and went to the door to listen for familiar footsteps upon the frozen ground. But no human form could be seen, as she gazed anxiously up the lane toward the village of N— S——, eight miles distant, where her husband had been tarrying too long.

The affectionate wife knew too well, alas! that her husband, whom she so fondly expected, was a drunkard; that the scornful finger of many a thoughtless one had often been pointed toward her own loved children, and that as often it had been said, "There goes a drunkard's child."

Six happy-hearted boys, and a healthful little girl, the youngest save one, gladdened the humble home of J— B———. For when he was sober, than he there never breathed a more noble-minded, loving father. Never a kinder hand than his ministered to the wants of a devoted wife and family. Yet he was a drunkard. It is a sad thought that intemperance claims its victims from among the noblest of the race. It reaches up to the purest mind and drags it down into utter ruin at last! Like thousands who feel their danger, but are too timorous to nerve themselves against it, this unfortunate man had not the moral courage to overcome the influences of his cunning enemy, the intoxicating cup. When he was uninfluenced by the spirit of the wine, he was social, intelligent, and generous to a fault. He seemed never so happy as when his children were around him, and his gentle wife by his side. Then they were indeed a happy family. And in these precious times of domestic enjoyment, many were the secret promises which that father would make to himself that never again should he abuse the love centred in him by those dear ones whom God had given him as objects worthy of the purest and tenderest regard the human heart can bestow. Many the tears silently wept over the manifold follies of a life so estranged as his had been, when the evil seducings of the tempter had drawn him away from home and love to mingle in the unhallowed society of the intemperate.

But solemn sorrow over the errors of the past, and penitential promises of reform for the future, seemed alike unavailing. Even when he trusted most in his own power of resistance, he would yield to temptation. His thirst for the burning beverage was more intense than his faith in promises, or trust in prayer, at the trying hour. And he yielded, as it were, to the allurements of the destroyer, in the very midst of warnings, and in spite of the earnest whisperings of his own conscience. When alcohol crazed his brain, he ceased to resemble a man, and spoke and acted as a demon. The ones he loved the most devotedly before, were now the hated of all the earth! His wife and children became the objects of his cruelty; and his voice once toned and softened with kindly words to all, now breathed curses upon his own flesh and blood!

Yet this broken-hearted wife, with all a true woman's devotedness, loved him notwithstanding all, and bore patiently his abuses. Although in his infatuation for drink, when his appetite was intensified by disease, he was known to take the very shoes from her feet and sell them for rum, and although he would drive his children sorrowing and supperless to miserable beds, yet that faithful wife loved him with a devotion that was more than human.

It was early in the morning of the day whose night was so cheerless and cold, when B—— started to the village. He had been industrious and contented for many weeks, and had saved a considerable amount of money from his earnings as a mechanic; and with so much to encourage and comfort her, his poor wife was elate with the hope that her husband was, indeed, reformed. Together they had planned for purchasing new clothes for their children, and some necessary articles of furniture for the house.

"And you shall have new shoes, and a nice dress, Sarah," he said to his wife that morning, with a voice so tender and loving that it brought memories of other and happier days.

"Never mind me, my dear," she replied, "get just what you think the children need most, and save something to buy yourself a new hat and a coat; and if you have enough left, you may bring me a cheap dress and a pair of coarse shoes, so we can go with the boys every Sabbath to the little church across the fields when spring comes again. I do think we shall have such happy times now. I always knew you wanted to be kind."

And so it was arranged that B—— should go to the village that day, and make some purchases in time to reach home before dark. He started early, kissing his companion as he bade her a short farewell, and was soon walking briskly over the hard, rough road toward the village. Then, as he hurried along, his thoughts were busy painting fanciful pictures of prosperity, and in his soul he resolved to live a temperate life evermore, not only for his own sake, but for the consolation of those who looked to him as their supporter and their all in this world.

How anxiously beat that mother's heart all that long day! She knew there was danger, for the vile tempter was ever vigilant, and would even deceive and destroy the father of her children—the sharer of her joys and her sorrows through all this life. Little Henry and Robert were delighted with the prospect of new clothes, so they could go to school where they met so many joys in their studies. Two more diligent scholars than they were not known in the old school-house where they attended school. Their lessons were always pleasant to them, and their recitations such as made the teacher claim them as favorite students; indeed, they were enthusiastic little fellows, and made many friends among all who knew them. If the children of the rich farmers would sometimes sadden these two young hearts by tossing out the saucy, "Your father's a drunkard," it would soon be forgotten and forgiven, marking its going away from remembrance by slight tear-tracks along their ruddy cheeks. Samuel, the eldest, a fine, manly boy of fourteen, tried to be happy that day; but the remembrance of the sorrows he had felt, the cruelties he had seen, and the imprecations he had heard, made him quiet and thoughtful.

When evening came at last without bringing home the expected father, the worst fears of Samuel and his mother began to show themselves in frequent sighs and fervent expressions of regret at his long absence.

"I do wish he would come," said Samuel, lifting his eyes from the fire, and looking through his tears into his mother's face, "Do you think he will come to-night, mother?"

"Yes, my son, I hope he will soon be here. Let us wait patiently. It is a long road in a cold, stormy night like this, and he must be very weary. We will try and keep the room warm and comfortable for him—he will be so tired and hungry, I know he will."

The night wore on, and he came not.

Often and often did Mrs. B—— go to the door and gaze out through the night in the direction from whence she longed to greet his coming. But she heard nothing, save the howling of the wind as it roared through the moonlit forests beyond the fields; she saw nothing, save the flying clouds, the tall trees bending to the swift winds, or falling to the frozen ground far out in the merciless storm.

\* \* \* \* \* \*

B—— finished his business in the village, and with his bundle of home gladdenings for his wife and little ones, had started on his return, tempted once or twice, it is true, by former associates in bacchanalian revelry, yet not deceived. He was almost ready to cry "*victory!*" over the one great enemy of his life, who had been so powerful in the warfare against his domestic peace, when, alas! he chanced to meet a social dram-drinker—one of those fashionable tipplers who lounge about the devil's dens on earth—one of those who never abuse *themselves*—oh, no! and on being urged by the wily flattery of this wretch to step aside into a saloon for a moment—only a moment—and take a friendly glass before starting on his long walk, he yielded, and thus made wreck of all his joys for ever! With the taste of the wine came the craving for more, and unable to stifle the desire, he bought a flask filled with this

"Dark beverage of Hell,"

of which to partake on his lonely, homeward way. At first, his step was light, and his heart joyous, as he hastily climbed the hill above the village, behind which his last sun was setting in the direction of his humble cottage home where a fond welcome was awaiting him. The first sip of the stimulating draught gave him momentary courage and strength for the journey, but the excess of the stimulus which the first taste invited, brought stupor upon his entire frame. Soon his weary body grew heavy and burdensome; and fevered within, and freezing without, he swayed to and fro along the dreary road, until at last, overcome by fatigue, the unfortunate man lay down on the ground to rest and to sleep, "perchance to dream."

His brain was wild with horrible fears; his heart was broken and bleeding within him; visions of laughing fiends haunted him continually; he groaned, he cried for help, but his cries were mocked by the night-winds; cold, slimy snakes crawled over his bed, coiled around his body, and hissed their fiery, forked tongues in his face; he dreamed he could hear his wife calling his name; he saw her waiting, and watching, and weeping for him; he tried to move toward her, but he was bound hand and foot by some invisible power, he knew not what; he felt the shackles of the tyrant on his hands, his feet, even around his very heart an iron-chain, all rusted over with tears, was fastened, and festering in his vitals; his eyes seemed burning and bursting from their sockets; his bones were cracking with cold; his blood gurgled from his veins, and froze in red icicles over his flesh! He lingered thus, suffering the most excruciating torments all that terrible night; and so near his own home, too, that in a calm, still evening his piteous cries could have been heard at his own fireside! But his almost distracted wife knew not that he had been so cruelly deceived, and was languishing his life away so near his home! She would have flown to his relief on wings of pity and compassion—unwearying wings that always lift the body of any angel of mercy over every obstacle, when commissioned to minister to the wants of suffering humanity everywhere. She would have pillowed his dying head upon her bosom out in the cold night, and perished with him there.

As Mrs. B—— drew the cottage door ajar that dismal night to watch for her beloved, she could see the swaying tops of the very tree by the road-side, beneath whose sighing branches her husband was then dreaming and dying in the agonies of delirium. It was a fearful death!

But the morning's sun shone out smilingly from the eastern skies, and the restless winds had ceased their revelings, when a neighbor passed that way and found a stiff and frozen corpse stretched by the road-side. There was the bundle of presents for his family whom he had not forgotten in his last resolve to be faithful and true, but to whom he was husband and father no more! And close by his side was the conqueror—the half-empty bottle, the remaining contents of which was the only unfrozen thing in all the sad ruin, as though it proved itself to be close kindred to the spirits of those regions infernal where all is everlasting burning.

When that ghastly form, once the loved father of those weeping, little children, and the cherished comforter of that now stricken widow, was taken home to await the preparation for burial, it was more than the disconsolate woman could endure. She wept as one for whom there was no more comfort—no more hope.

The grave received its new victim with a welcome, and he was covered deep and alone for his long rest. Not until the judgment day will those lips that so often tasted the wine, be parted to curse or to confess; but *then* they will move once more, when the great burden of a life's sorrows will be spoken by the drunkard, and the penalty be inflicted not only on the unfortunate inebriate, but likewise on the one who suffered less in this life—the vender of the poison—whose sin is greater in the sight of just Heaven. And when comes the vender's terrible judgment, then will the whole truth be told before the great assizes of the recompensing Judge of all, and the *legalizer* of the traffic in intoxicating drink will hear the severest doom that stands affixed to any violated law of God. Oh, save the living from incurring that awful sentence!

The widow never recovered from her deep afflict: It was too much for her sensitive, delicate nature, a she sunk beneath the weight of her troubles. In a f months she died of grief, far away from the scene of he many trials, even in the midst of friends. She was laid to rest in a beautiful cemetery. Hers is a Christian's grave; and when her honored dust shall be gathered into living flesh "in the twinkling of an eye," when the archangel's trump shall sound down from the Judgment Throne of Jehovah, her pale lips will praise the Lord for so soft a slumber, and shout aloud at the opening of the golden gates of so sweet a heaven, as she hears the welcome, " Well done—enter into the joys of thy Lord!"

Heaven has befriended the orphans. And may those who fear no danger, think of the many who have fallen!

# WINTER.

'Tis winter, and the cold winds moan
   Through all the Northern lands;
The streams are fastened, every one,
   In icy fetter-bands.
      So shall the wintry air of death
         Congeal our flowing tears,
      And chill our life-blood, stop our breath,
         And end our trial years.

The crystal snow, so pure and light,
   Is sifted to the ground;
The fields and forests, sprinkled white,
   No more with mirth resound.
      So shall a white and spotless shroud
         Our mortal forms enfold,
      When these young hearts of ours, so proud,
         In death are still and cold.

The gentle birds have gone away
   To sing in orange groves;
And there, O, sweetly all the day,
   They tell their tender loves!
      So Death—our spirits then shall stay
         In heavenly bowers so fair,
      And sweetly sing, and dove-like play
         Among the laurels there.

# VALLEY FORGE.

EARLY in the morning of a chilly day toward the close of November, 1860, we started on the comfortable cars of the Philadelphia and Reading Railroad, bound for a day's ramble along the banks of the romantic Schuylkill. In about an hour after our departure from the city of Brotherly Love, we arrived at the secluded dale at the mouth of Valley Creek, distant twenty miles north-west from the city, known on the page of our country's history, and in the sad remembrances of those who there exhibited true patriotic devotion, as VALLEY FORGE—a name dear to every American heart.

The forest trees that stood in clusters on the hill-slopes on either side of the valley, had already shaken off their summer foliage, and were bared to the cold winds that moaned sad autumn-farewells through their desolate branches. The fields had assumed the dull, dead brown that frosts bring in exchange for the living green of summer. The sky was leaden, and the atmosphere damp and disagreeable. The day was peculiarly appropriate for visiting the scenes of suffering and of sorrow, such as were here endured by the noble faithful of the "times that tried men's souls."

The river curves a little to the left as you ascend its

western shore, on which side it receives the waters of Valley Creek, a meandering little stream that drains a fertile and extensive slope stretching off to the westward.

This celebrated spot takes its name from an iron forge, located in the vicinity, which belonged to one Isaac Potts, a Friend, who called these lands his own even before the time of the Revolution. Valley Creek is sufficiently large to drive the great water-wheel of a large cotton factory which stands upon the site of the old forge, and adjacent to the junction of the two streams. The residence of Isaac Potts, situated near the mouth of the creek, is a substantial, but old-fashioned stone building, and is occupied to this day as a dwelling. In this same house Washington had a small private room in which he attended to his correspondence, and held social intercourse with his officers. In the sill of the east window, is an ingenious little cavity in which the Commander-in-chief deposited his important papers. A casual observer would never suspect any such hidden depository, for the rough carpentry is so adjusted that the innocent timber upon which you lean to admire the landscape without, has the appearance of an ordinary sill—and nothing more!

From this window the visitor obtains a fine view of the ·hallowed hills around; the ruins of the old flour-mill, whose hum was heard in that peaceful valley long before the roar of the cannons made those regions the place of strife and the camping grounds of brave warriors; and here, too, the eye may follow the many crooks and ripples of the little creek, as it comes down from the high lands, off toward the Brandywine, waving and sparkling like a silver ribbon flung out over the brown vesture of the meadows.

We wandered leisurely up to the summit of the hill on the south, at which elevation the main part of the American army was quartered. The lodging places of the soldiers were nearly all rude cabins, hastily built and very low and small. The deep snows of that terrible winter so nearly covered them altogether that they had the appearance of mere burrows in the drifts! Just on the spot where General Washington's marquee was situated, there now stands a beautiful observatory, about forty feet in hight. Here we had a general view of the entire camping ground and all the picturesque surroundings of Valley Forge. It is a lovely landscape, even in dreary November; but historical associations intensify the thrilling emotions that swell the heart on beholding these eventful grounds. Here, in the melancholy winter of 1777–8, our forefathers suffered the bitter bitings of the cold and the tedious tortures of famine. Poor soldiers! what trials they endured! Proud patriots! what liberties they purchased for us! When the army marched from Whitemarsh to Valley Forge, it is said that their bloody foot-prints were distinctly visible in the snow for nineteen miles!

Benson J. Lossing, the historian and traveler, upon visiting this spot, eloquently observed: "How dear to the true worshiper at the shrine of Freedom is the name of Valley Forge! Here, in the midst of frost and snow, disease and destitution, Liberty erected her altar; and in all the world's history we have no record of purer devotion, holier sincerity, or more pious self-sacrifice, than was here exhibited in the camp of Washington.

## VALLEY FORGE. 273

The courage that nerves the arm on the battle-field, and dazzles by its brilliant but evanescent flashes, pales before the steadier and more intense flame of patient endurance, the sum of the sublime heroism displayed at Valley Forge. And if there is a spot on the face of the broad land whereon Patriotism should delight to pile its highest and most venerated monument, it should be in the bosom of that little vale on the bank of the Schuylkill."

There is a touching incident connected with the history of Valley Forge. One day, when the disconsolate army were almost ready to despair, when starvation stared them in the face, and when their weary bodies were well nigh worn out with cold and fatigue, Isaac Potts, who was a preacher in the society of Friends, happened to pass along through the camp, and heard the many lamentations, and beheld the many tears, but could only sympathize with them in his heart, and hope with them for the dawning of a better day. He passed on, sorrowing and thoughtful, into the dark forest farther up the creek, where all was silent as the grave. There were no birds to sing and flutter among the groves; no insects to relieve the deep quiet; no breeze murmured through the leafless trees. There was not a single, solitary sound in all the forest valley whither he wandered, when, suddenly, he noticed Washington's horse tied to the swinging limb of a tree. He paused to listen, when, lo! from a thicket of evergreens, near at hand, came a voice, sad and solemn. It was the Commander-in-chief upon his knees engaged in humble, penitential prayer! His eyes were raised to heaven, and his cheeks suffused with tears. Potts was much excited at so strange a spectacle, and feeling that he had ventured on holy ground, cautiously withdrew from the place without attracting observation from the Christian warrior. When he reached his home below the camp, he burst into tears, and remarked to his agitated wife, who had never seen her husband so deeply affected, that, " If there is any one on this earth whom the Lord will listen to, it is George Washington; and I feel a presentiment that under such a commander there can be no doubt of our establishing our independence, and that God in his providence has willed it so."

What a mighty power—borrowed strength from the God of battles! And such was Washington's faith, that this influence was vouchsafed to him by the arm of the Almighty! No wonder he conquered! The hosts of heaven were marshaled on the right and on the left of the chief, and thus our land was redeemed. And thus may it be ever preserved from foreign agression, or from sectional strife! Let disunionists remember Valley Forge, and Washington's close communion with the Great Father of us all.

> "O, who shall know the might
> Of the words he uttered there;
> The fate of nations there was turned,
> By the fervor of his prayer.
>
> "But wouldst thou know his name,
> Who wandered there alone?
> Go, read enrolled in heaven's archives
> *The prayer of* WASHINGTON!"

As we strolled up the valley alone toward the evening, it seemed like enchanted ground; for here are the ancient trees, and, perchance, beneath this very old hemlock whose dark green branches intermingle with the evergreen boughs of adjoining pines, forming a ceiling of foliage, and casting a solemn shade through the wide, dim aisles of the wood, here in this secluded retreat, may have been the identical place where our country's chieftain knelt and prayed. And from this sacred shrine in this, one of

<blockquote>"God's first temples,"</blockquote>

earnest prayer ascended to the heavenly Throne, and here came down sweet assurances that prayer *does* reach the ear of Jehovah. Oh, it seemed a precious privilege to stand upon that honored, that consecrated ground! It seemed an easy place to pray now, since prayer was answered there; and the heart's thanksgivings went up unconsciously, borne on wings of love and gratitude, that this land of ours is still one and undivided.

Would that every one, this day, who lightly esteems our glorious Union of States, might, pilgrim-like and penitent, peace-loving and prayerful, repair to the silent shades of Valley Forge, and there renew his vows to maintain inviolate this threatened Confederacy!

We left Valley Forge just as the sun, all curtained with gorgeous gold, was sinking to his bed, behind the western hills. Our meditations were sad, yet pleasing—sad to remember what sufferings were here endured for our sake—pleased to think that our country is free, and that the war for Independence was so triumphantly ended.

Strangers visiting Philadelphia on pleasure, should not

fail to devote one day, at least, to an excursion along the banks of the Schuylkill. An hour's ride on the cars, through a region of varied and beautiful scenery along the meandering river, will take the visitor to the camp-ground at Valley Forge.

## TIPPECANOE.

In all the great West there is not a richer or more beautiful region than the valley of the Wabash in Indiana. It was a lovely morning in the month of June, when we arrived at Lafayette, a busy little city in Tippecanoe county, on our homeward route from Kentucky, by way of the Louisville, New Albany, and Chicago Railroad, which extends from the Ohio River to Lake Michigan, and passes through some of the most fertile portions of the State. The Superintendent of the Road, R. E. Ricker, Esq., is a gentleman whom we shall ever remember for his many kindnesses.

Ascertaining that the celebrated Battle Ground of Tippecanoe was but a few miles farther north, immediately on the line of the Railroad, we resolved at once to visit the spot. But as the next train of cars in that direction would not be due for several hours, and knowing that our time was limited to that single day in that portion of the State, we found it would be necessary to hire a private conveyance, or else go afoot, to the Battle Ground, where there would be ample time to make observations before the arrival of the first train bound for the lake-end of the State. We chose the latter mode of travel, and were soon on our solitary way, stepping over the "ties" of the Road, beneath a hot summer's sun, from whose scorching rays our umbrella was but a flimsy shelter.

Almost any arrangement of terrestrial surface affords a more comfortable promenade to a pedestrian than the unballasted track of a railroad. The cross-ties to which the iron rails are fastened, are just a trifle too close together to gauge ordinary steppings; and to step on every alternate one, is about two-trifles-and-a-half too long a stride for graceful walking. However, as on most such thoroughfares, there was a smooth and inviting little foot-path close along-side the main track, and in some places, occupying for a few furlongs a kind of *betweenity*, with an iron rail on either side. This was its location more especially where the ties were partially covered by the black loam of the valley. There was a blending of two roads here, one the great iron highway for the ponderous engine and its mighty train of swift and roaring cars, burdened with the products of the thousand fertile fields, or with hundreds of human beings; the other, a tiny, narrow path, bordered with delicate flowers and fringed with verdure, whereon were tracks of little bare feet which had hurried to the summer school! Along this humble path we journeyed for two hours through extensive meadows of tall grass, wide fields of blossoming clover, or broad acres of young corn in which the farmers were busy that day plowing and hoeing the promise of a great harvest. Here and there we observed a fine horse in harness, at rest or grazing in the shade of a mulberry tree, numbers of which stood at refreshing intervals throughout the vast cornfield.

The hills on either side of the river are low and densely covered, from their summits even down to the water's edge, with trees and bushes; the young leaves forming on the distant slopes, a comely vesture of living green which rustled in the gentle breeze as if dame Nature were really vain of her gay attire.

Leaving the cultivated bottom lands, we crossed the Wabash on a long wooden bridge, elevated some thirty feet from the surface of the water. Beyond the bridge, which is located about midway between Lafayette and the Battle Ground, the railroad diverges from the river, and leads through a forest in which we observed a preponderance of white-oak, walnut, locust, and beech timber. Just as we were leaving the bridge, and were about entering the woodland, we chanced to see an Irishman shading himself behind his rude shanty, at a little distance from the roadside. Desiring some information in regard to the probable distance to the place of our destination, and wishing to engage in a social conversation for a moment, even for the sake of making a new acquaintance by the way, we accosted him, "How far to the Battle Ground at Tippecanoe, sir, if you please?"

"Sir-r?"

"How far to Tippecanoe?"

"No sir-r—whin iver we's would be afther goin' achross, we can ford the river below, jist, or ilse we wak oover on the bridge, ayther. Yes, indade, sir-r, we *would* be afraid ov *tippen* over in a *canoe*, sir, an' it's well ye may say that!"

Not feeling quite certain whether Pat had ever heard of Tippecanoe, or whether he meant to amuse himself at our expense, we thought it best to quiz him no more, and thanking him for the information he afforded us, we passed on.

The woods in June! How full of music! how rich in beauty! how redolent in fragrance! The birds sang from every bough; the leaves laughed and whispered, and whispered and laughed, the little fairy flirts!—at every innocent zephyr that murmured through the groves; the odors of a thousand opening flowers made the air sweet and invigorating as it came into the lungs pure and fresh from heaven. There is an exhilarating influence that comes right home to the heart, when we linger in the dear old woods, and let our thoughts wander off amidst the leaves, or down to the gorgeous wild flowers that skirt the margin of the quiet river, or away up among the singing birds, to take lessons of love and content from the carols they sing all the day long. Such soul excursions are always blessed. Our walk through the woods of Wabash valley was one of peculiar delight, and its tender teachings are cherished memories still.

Soon we approached Tippecanoe River, a small stream coming down from the prairies of the north. The railroad leaves the main valley at the bridge above alluded to, and crosses the Tippecanoe River some two miles from its confluence with the Wabash. We were now in sight of the great Battle Ground. Immediately before us, on a little rise of woodland to the left of the road, is a grassy ridge running parallel to the little river at its base, and thickly set with oaks. That is the Battle Ground. A neat wooden fence surrounds an area of some ten acres, and in this enclosure, then an unbroken wilderness, on the memorable 7th of November, 1811, the great battle was fought.

It was a desperate struggle. On the one side were the whites, many of whose relatives and friends had been murdered by the enemy now concealed by hundreds in their very midst. And these cruel outrages were now to be avenged. There was no claim for pity, no desire for reconciliation on the part of the brave soldiers of Harrison. The foe was now within reach, and must be vanquished.

On the other side were the savage and persecuted citizens of the forest. They felt the whites to be the aggressors, coming in pomp and power to drive them from their rivers and hunting-grounds. Such an enemy, seeking their lands and their lives, the Indians were resolved to defeat and destroy, even to the bitter end. All their savage nature was aroused, and they determined to conquer or die in the attempt. It was a life-struggle with them, and they were wild with hatred toward the pale faces, and thirsted for their blood.

Many different tribes were confederated in this war against the whites. Tecumseh, a Shawnee chief, was the leader in uniting the tribes of the Northwest in opposition to the people of the United States, although he was not present in the battle, and took no part in the engagement. The loss was heavy on both sides; but victory turned in favor of the whites, and the Indians were, at length, completely routed. Here General Harrison distinguished himself as a warrior, and the name "Tippecanoe" associated with him ever after, even down to the time of his election to the Presidency, in 1840. The appellation was uttered in campaign speeches, and echoed in song throughout the land.

Now these western lands are the homes of thousands

of noble freemen, recognized as a part of the nation's best citizens—the farmers of Indiana. School-houses and dwellings almost innumerable have taken the places of the Indian wigwams of other years. Where once the wild war-whoop rang through the dark forests, now are heard the hymns of Christian love and fellowship. A very fine Academy stands on the battle-ground, in which institution we spent a pleasant hour among the teachers and pupils.

All happy days soon come to a close, and in the evening we were on our way northward to the distant prairie-lands, feeling that riding on a rail, however disreputable it may appear, is better than walking on ties, when speed and comfort are to be estimated in the traveler's book of accounts.

# YELLOW CREEK.

About fifty miles below the city of Pittsburgh, on the western shore of the Ohio, there is an abrupt promontory jutting out toward the river, close around the southern base of which winds a sparkling little stream until it blends its waters with the great river.

Some ten rods above the mouth of the creek, a meandering brook comes down a deep and narrow glen from the northward, parallel with the river, and mingles its pure waters, first with the creek, and then with the broad Ohio. The brook, the creek, and the river form three boundaries, in almost right-angular lines to the high hill between. The smallest of these three streams is known in all that region as "Block House Run," from the fact that a fort was here erected in early times as a defence against the Indians.

To the non-observant traveler who chances to pass that way, there may be nothing very remarkable in the place, yet it must present striking peculiarities to any one who will but for a moment glance at the scenery which here meets the eye.

At this point the railroad diverges from the river, and passes up the valley of the creek until at length it gains the more elevated plains off toward Cleveland.

Another branch of the railroad extends along the river shore, passing sweet Woodbine Cottage, the home of the children's friend, "UNCLE EDWARD," and connects with western continuations of rail, both at Steubenville, seventeen miles below, and also at Bellair, nearly opposite Wheeling.

A high and substantial bridge spans the creek, near its junction with the river; and a few rods farther up the stream, is the old covered bridge, so near the water that in time of a high freshet the structure is submerged half way to its roof. The main line of the railroad passes directly through the rocky point, and the overhanging precipice above has the appearance of an immense mountain-side of bare sand-stone, ragged-edged and roughed by the blastings which hewed it down for the laying of the iron rails at its base. A small frame station-house, unpainted and weather-beaten, stands at the foot of the declivity, close between the two divisions of the railroad, so that the traveler may step from its eastern porch into the river-train, or from its western door into the train for the Forest City, on Lake Erie.

On the other side of the creek is an elevated plain on which stood an Indian village in the days of Logan, the distinguished Mingo Chief. On the Virginia side of the Ohio, directly opposite the mouth of Yellow Creek, occurred the notorious massacre of the Indians by Colonel Cresap, on the 24th May, 1774. Among the slain were a brother and daughter of Logan. It was a cold-blooded murder on the part of the whites, although they subsequently made many excuses in justification of their heartless conduct.

This exasperated the savages, and a long and bloody

war followed, the desolating influences of which were felt throughout the West. Sometime afterward, Logan delivered his celebrated speech, in which he excused himself for his intense hatred toward the white man.

About two miles below, on the eastern shore of the Ohio, is the scene of Adam Poe's thrilling adventure with Big-foot, the Indian warrior. The identical spot where the pioneer made his daring leap upon his foe, has been frequently pointed out to the writer by an old settler who was accurately informed, and who still resides in the vicinity.

But these memorable events have been faithfully recorded on the page of history. We allude to them thus casually, to evidence to the reader that the subject of our sketch is not entirely devoid of interesting and important historical associations.

Passing up the fertile valley of the creek three or four miles, the traveler is in the midst of one of the richest coal regions west of the Alleghanies. The high hills, and deep ravines, on every hand, are wildly romantic. In winter, when the clustered hemlocks along the shores, and the scattered and desolate pines farther up the slopes, are foliaged in evergreen, and when the hill-tops are crested with snow, the effect produced by the contrast is enchanting. Or, in summer-time, when the forest trees are decorated with leaves, and the woodlands are musical with birds; when the meadows and fields down in the winding valleys are luxuriant in their growths of grass and corn, the beholder may well take delight in rambling along the shores of Yellow Creek!

While others may talk in raptures of the majestic

Hudson, sing the praises of the "Blue Juniata," wander in silent admiration along the tuneful Tennessee, or weave fanciful stories of fairies and angel-loiterers in a thousand "Sleepy Hollows" elsewhere in our broad domain, we remember our dear old Yellow Creek as the place of our earliest hopes and our purest joys. Near its rippling waters stands the Old Log School House, a few of whose experiences we have attempted to relate on the first pages of this little volume; and were we so disposed, we could tell many a strange tale of wondrous deeds oft-times rehearsed at the humble fireside, years and years ago, by the story-tellers who would linger beneath the cabin-roof of our early home on Yellow Creek hills. One somewhat dim on memory's tablet we shall attempt to narrate.

A long time ago, before any of the pioneers had permanently settled in the valley of Yellow Creek, it was common for Virginians to make excursions over these hills, bringing their horses with them from the settlements, and hobbling them in the wild meadows to graze, while they wandered off in search of game in which the woods abounded. In such exploits it was usual to sleep on the grass with the far-off sky as the only shelter, and the distant howlings of the wolves the only lullaby.

About this time, salt springs were discovered on the creek, and rude furnaces were built for "boiling salt." The persons who first engaged in this business were a daring, reckless class of men, not particularly regardful of their appearance or habits. Commonly, two or three would join fortunes, erect a rough cabin, and build a furnace near a saline spring, there to spend weeks and months boiling salt in the wilderness.

One of these establishments was owned and operated by a rough, mischievous fellow by the name of Miller, who was always ready for a joke, no matter how severe, or at whose expense. While Miller, and his two associates in the enterprise, were seated around the great roaring furnace one morning, wishing for some kind of amusement, a stranger, lean and lank, having every symptom of a genuine Vermonter, approached on horseback, and asked permission to leave his pack-saddle and other traveling appendages in their care, while he should spend the day in hunting. The favor being cheerfully granted, he dismounted, left his saddle, and wandered off in quest of deer.

As soon as the new-comer was fairly out of sight, Miller, who looked upon him as an intruder, determined to annoy him; and as a convenient method of testing the calibre of the stranger, he threw his pack-saddle into the furnace where it was soon reduced to ashes. Toward evening the hunter returned, and on very deliberately making inquiry for his saddle, was told the less he said about that the better, otherwise *he* might share the same fate. The remark was accompanied by a significant look toward the fire, which instantly suggested to the indignant stranger the whereabouts of his saddle. However, he said nothing, and was soon on his homeward way.

In a few days he returned once more, seeming in a fine humor, and brought a new pack-saddle which he left in Miller's care, as before, charging him emphatically not to burn *that* one, or else there would be a *noise* about it. Of course, the warning not to touch the saddle was more than Miller was willing to bear, and he resolved to repeat the experiment as soon as the stranger should start on his day's hunt. No sooner had he turned his back upon the furnace, than Miller called after him—

"Look-a-here, Mister, I'll show you who's a goin' to do the *orderin'* round here," and into the fire went the saddle with a will! But in a moment the huge kettles, the walls of the furnace, and every thing thereunto pertaining, were scattered in one universal wreck, the hot fluid sprinkling freely over the unsuspecting heads of the salt-boilers, and the clouds of hissing steam completely blinding them for a while, thus affording the revengeful stranger opportunity to make good his escape, which he did without the formality of bidding his victims "good-bye!" The truth flashed upon Miller's mind, about as soon as the hot ashes flashed into his face—*the pads of the new pack-saddle had been stuffed with gun powder!*

www.ingramcontent.com/pod-product-compliance
Lightning Source LLC
Chambersburg PA
CBHW032047230426
43672CB00009B/1510